FOUL DEEDS AND SUSPICIOUS DEATHS
IN CUMBRIA

TRUE CRIME FROM WHARNCLIFFE

Foul Deeds and Suspicious Deaths Series

OTHER TRUE CRIME BOOKS FROM WHARNCLIFFE

Please contact us via any of the methods below for more information
or a catalogue
WHARNCLIFFE BOOKS
47 Church Street, Barnsley, South Yorkshire, S70 2AS
Tel: 01226 734555 • 734222 • Fax: 01226 734438
email: enquiries@pen-and-sword.co.uk
website: www.wharncliffebooks.co.uk

Foul Deeds & Suspicious Deaths in
CUMBRIA

Nicholas Corder

Wharncliffe Books

First published in Great Britain in 2008 by
Wharncliffe Books
an imprint of
Pen and Sword Books Limited,
47 Church Street, Barnsley,
South Yorkshire. S70 2AS

Copyright © Nicholas Corder, 2008

ISBN: 978 1 845630 65 2

A CIP catalogue record of this book is available from the
British Library.

Typeset in Plantin and Benguiat by
Pen and Sword Books Ltd

Printed in the United Kingdom by
CPI UK

Pen & Sword Books Ltd incorporates the imprints of
Pen & Sword Aviation, Pen & Sword Maritime,
Pen & Sword Military, Wharncliffe Local History, Pen & Sword Select,
Pen & Sword Military Classics, Leo Cooper, Remember When, Seaforth Publishing
and Frontline Publishing

For a complete list of Pen & Sword titles please contact:
PEN & SWORD BOOKS LIMITED
47 Church Street, Barnsley, South Yorkshire, S70 2AS, England.
E-mail: enquiries@pen-and-sword.co.uk
Website: www.pen-and-sword.co.uk

Contents

Acknowledgements

everal people helped in the writing of this book. The library staff of Kendal, and the staff at Preston, Whitehaven, Barrow and Carlisle archives have been as helpful as it is possible to be. Many thanks to them.

Tracey from Essex and Tony March put up (with) the travelling researchers as did Wadvern Davies, whilst Lesley Harris fed us. Keith Thomas not only ferreted out some stuff we had missed at the archives in Whitehaven, but paid for lunch as well. George Stewart of Burneside also dug up the tail-end of a case for us when we had run out of time in Kendal. Without them, two of the stories in this book wouldn't have made it into print. Ivor Davies read the manuscript looking for silly mistakes, so we all know who to blame if we find any.

Lastly, as ever, huge amounts of the research and typing were done by my wife, Pauline, who really should get a co-credit, but I like to keep all the royalties for myself. All photographs in this book are by the author.

Lancaster Castle. The castle served as gaol and assizes. Thomas Donahoo (Chapter 10), John Stainton (Chapter 9) and the suspects in the Trades Union murder (Chapter 15) all appeared here.

Introduction

Cumbria is one of those counties created by the re-organisation of local government in 1974. Its formation meant that Westmorland 'disappeared', that parts of Lancashire on the northern fringes of Morecambe Bay, as well as some places that until that point had been happily part of the Yorkshire Ridings for generations, were sucked into the new conglomerate county.

Cumbria is Britain's third largest county, covering an area of over 6,700 square kilometers. Whilst for many outside the area, it is most famous for the Lake District, the region has a long industrial past. Long before the part now beloved of hikers and ramblers was made famous by Wordsworth and his druggy chums, it was an area of mines and small factories. Up until very recently, the towns on the coast were characterised by iron and steel works, shipbuilding, fishing and the chemicals industry. As manufacturing has moved to where labour is cheaper, or replacement technologies require fewer human beings, so too these towns have suffered. Many of the larger towns are still rebuilding themselves and looking for a new rôle in the modern cyber-age. We used to have industry; now we have industrial museums.

Look up the area now known as Cumbria in Domesday and you will see that the book's coverage stops somewhere slightly north of Millom. Large swathes of the northern half of the county changed hands between Scots and English for generations, making Cumberland the Alsace-Lorraine of Britain. In this border country, known as the Debatable Lands, terrible deeds of theft, rape, murder and violence took place as families each side of the border took it in turns to avenge outrages. Who started it all has long been lost in the midst of time, but it was a land of lawlessness. These tribal factions were known as the Border Reivers (apparently a variation on the word 'ruffian'). It would take the Act of Union of 1703 to fix borders and put an end to the shenanigans. The Pele Towers which can still be found today are a legacy of that era, when the wealthier families kept their sheep in pens inside mini-fortresses built specifically to keep a watch over the surrounding countryside.

Judges' Lodgings, Lancaster. Between 1776 and 1975, this house was used by the visiting judges presiding over the assizes at the nearby castle.

As the area was administered by three different counties, the Assizes for many of these crimes were held in Carlisle (for Cumberland), Lancaster (for the Cartmel and Furness peninsulas) and Appleby for the few crimes that happened in the Westmorland area.

All three towns are today well-kept and inviting, and whilst, like anywhere, they still have a few problems, the average visitor would have little to complain about. *The Times* of 19 August 1818 was very complimentary about Appleby, although less flattering about its inhabitants:

> *Appleby is a very neat little town, and beautifully situated on a peninsula formed by a sweep of the Eden. The ground rises precipitously from the bank of the river to the neck of the peninsula, where it is very high, and where the castle is situated. The surrounding scenery is extremely romantic. The county of Westmorland is inland and agricultural. Its want of sea-port towns, and its want of commerce, have undoubtedly contributed to protect it from many crimes and offences. But the same causes have perpetuated, if not generated, an amazing degree of lethargy and*

stupidity among the people. In their assemblies, not a symptom of vivacity or ingenuity ever betrays itself. Frequent contests at elections might do much good. The collision might rub off a little of their incrusted rusticity. But for a while, their dogged and unreasoning obstinacy must render elections among them unreasonably disagreeable.

The English press then, as today, thought of the world as a series of spokes in a wheel whose axle was London. Although, the account is correct in at least one respect. Cumbria is not, and never has been, a hot-bed of criminals; whether that is because it is remote and therefore less prone to actual crimes, or that the remoteness means that you can commit crimes without fear of detection, who can tell. However, the inhabitants of large parts of the rest of our small island must look in envy at the crime figures for the region.

Cumbria, possibly because of its 'incrusted rusticity' remains one of the safest places in the country and its inhabitants past and present, largely law-abiding. Of course, there are exceptions and some of them can be found in this book, although not every foul deed in this book was perpetrated by a Cumbrian! Since the English and the Scots stopped nicking one another's sheep, things have calmed down a lot in the north of the country.

Nonetheless, contained in these pages are swindlers, conmen, rapists and murderers. In amongst those who acted for their own

The Citadel, Carlisle. The building has been used as the courts and prison since the early 1800s. Several of the characters in this book passed through here.

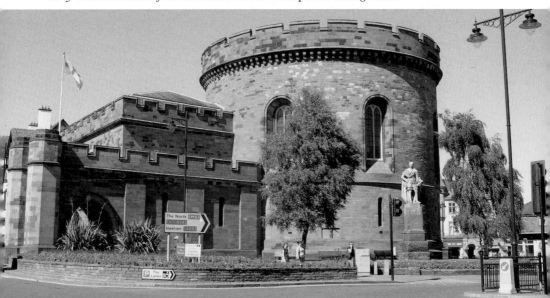

'Hanging Corner', Lancaster Castle. Murderers from all over Lancashire were brought here to hang. Of the people in this book, Thomas Donahoo from Ulverston probably came nearest to being hanged here.

gain are plenty of ordinary people who killed out of desperation, drunkenness, madness or because a meanness of spirit was allowed to flourish for whatever reason.

Remember that the person from whom you are most in danger is the one with whom you share a bed! So, if there's one piece of advice that you should take away from this book, it's that you must be very careful indeed whose bed you share.

Chapter 1

John Paul Jones and the Whitehaven Raid 1778

He was the commander, so he was first into the fort. They didn't need the scaling ladders. Instead they stood on the shoulders of the biggest men in the landing party and broke through to capture the small group of look-outs manning the half-moon battery, stunned by the sudden presence of armed raiders.

These look-outs were supposed to be in charge of the thirty-six guns, fanned in an arc, pointing into the feeble light of an April dawn. These were the guns that were supposed to protect the harbour of Whitehaven. They weren't going to defend anywhere tonight.

He had divided his landing party of three officers and twenty-nine men into two groups. Whilst he and his men were on the south side, silencing the guns, the other group in the smaller boat would by now be in place in the harbour itself. Lieutenant Samuel Wallingsford and Midshipman Ben Hill were in charge of this second group. They carried bits of canvas, dipped in brimstone, which they planned to set alight and throw onto the decks or amongst the rigging of the boats of large fleet that lay at rest in the harbour.

The commander of the raid was a small, fiery, red-headed Scot called John Paul Jones. He was daring, intrepid and ruthlessly ambitious to rise as far as he could above his humble beginnings as a gardener's son. He had, through a succession of adventures that had seen him serve on all kinds of merchant ships including slavers, found his way to America. As America geared itself for war against Britain, so Jones found his niche. Now he was Captain of *The Ranger*.

A modern day statue showing one of John Paul Jones's men spiking the guns at Whitehaven.

Jones had spent the previous fortnight sailing the sloop from Brest towards the Irish Sea looking for opportunities to engage the British in battle. According to his own memoirs, he was ready to raid England on 17 April, but he was blown off course and found himself off the coast of Ireland. Here, he happened upon a British frigate, HMS *Drake*, in the port of Carrickfergus. He made plans to capture the frigate, but according to Ezra Green, the ship's surgeon, the crew was unwilling to do so before dark. When they attempted to do so after nightfall, the mate had according to Jones 'drunk too much brandy, did not drop the anchor at the instant the order was given to him' and the chance of capture was gone.

A few days after the aborted raid on Carrickfergus, Jones recorded in his memoirs that he attempted 'a second time to descend on England' – a plan that greatly alarmed his lieutenants: 'Their object,' they said, 'was gain not honour.' They were poor: instead of encouraging the morale of the crew, they excited them to disobedience; they persuaded them that they had the right to judge whether a measure that was proposed to them was good or bad.'

In those days, crews were dependent for their money on ships they captured or sank and a raid on a town like Whitehaven would have merely put their lives in danger without any chance of making any money from it.

It was now the night of 22-23 April 1778, and Jones found himself opposite the harbour at Whitehaven – a town he knew well. It was here that John Paul (as he then was) came in about 1761 as a lad of thirteen or fourteen, signing papers of apprenticeship to John Younger, a prominent local trader and civic dignitary. Over the next few years, he was to make at least four trips from Whitehaven to the Caribbean and Virginia, with cargoes of pig iron, barrel staves, salt, rum and sugar depending on the leg of the voyage.

Whitehaven Harbour as it is today.

Whitehaven had grown prosperous from the power of Britain as a sea-faring nation and from the richness of the minerals under the Cumbrian soil. The commercial possibilities brought about by the opening up of the 'new lands' of the Americas and the Caribbean to the West turned the port of Whitehaven, which also included the harbours along the Cumberland coast at Millom, Workington and Maryport, into one of the five most important ports in England. By the mid-eighteenth century, the newly-planned Georgian town of Whitehaven, the first planned town since the Middle Ages, was a wealthy sea-port in what was then the world's wealthiest nation.

Jones, flushed with the success of his capture of the fort, then found that Wallingsford's boat had returned to the southern half of the harbour without achieving anything. 'Those who manned it,' he writes in his memoirs, 'pretended to have been intimidated by certain noises they had heard.'

Wallingsford's group had failed to carry out Jones's orders to fire the shipping in the harbour. They preferred the lure of the alehouse. The *Cumberland Chronicle* in a special edition described the events thus:

On Thursday morning, about two o'clock, 20 men, together with the Captain, landed on the battlement near the head of the Old Quay, from a boat belonging to the said vessel (which proves to be the Ranger American privateer, from Nantz, then standing off and on about two miles from this Harbour), whilst another boat came into the Harbour, and landed 10 men at the Old Quay flip, when they proceeded to Nick Allison's, a public house, on the Old Quay; they made very free with the liquors, &c. and would not permit any of the family, to stir out; after which a party went on board the Thompson, Capt Johnson's, a coal loaden vessel, lying opposite to Allison's took the boys out of bed, and set her on fire: They offered money to the boys to induce them to go with them, but on their refusing they put them under guard on the Quay, without any other covering than their shirts; having handkerchiefs tied over their mouths to prevent their crying out, at the same time the privateer's people threatening to shoot them if they made any noise or resistance. Immediately after the alarm was effectually given, the fire engines were brought to the Quay, and by the various exertions of people of all ranks, the fire on board the Thompson was speedily extinguished, without damaging any other vessel; thus were the malicious attempts of those daring incendiaries frustrated. Lighted matches, made of canvas dipped in brimstone, had been thrown on board several other vessels, but had gone out without having the intended effect.

The privateer's people were all armed with pistols and cutlasses, and retired to their boats about four o'clock (taking with them two boys, one from the Thompson and the other from the Saltham). They had, on their first landing, spiked several of the cannon, in order to secure their retreat. A number of people flocking to the forts, some shot were fired at the boats, but without doing any execution. After the boats reached the privateer, she stood over to the Scotch side, and as large columns of smoke have been seen on the Scotch shore this afternoon it is feared that she has done some mischief there.

Jones, it has to be pointed out, was not a privateer, nor even a pirate, as many tried to make out at the time. By modern standards, he would be what one would call a 'traitor', although that again depends on which side of the Atlantic Ocean you hail from. He was also pretty much disliked by all his crew, who were used to a more democratic style of leadership than that of the monomaniacal Jones.

Not only were half his crew engaged in some early morning drinking, but one crew member, David Freeman, took the opportunity to desert and to raise the alarm amongst the townsfolk.

In a last ditch effort to fire the fleet, Jones and the men in his party dropped their lighted canvas rags onto the decks of a few ships in the south side of the harbour, before clambering back into their boats and pulling away from the shore.

The ship's log records the events of the day thus:

This 24 hours begins with fresh gales and squally. TKt. Ship to ye Eastward Tkt. Ship to ye Westward out all Refs rigg'd both top gallant yards at 7 Takt. Ship to ye Eastward Whitehaven Light bore SE1/2E Dis 7 leagues at 12 was abrest of Whitehaven hover Two the Captn and 40 men went on shore and Spiked up all the Guns in the Two Forts and Sett fire to the shipping at Day Light Returned on board in Boats and made sail.

Coming off in a hurry left one man, David Smith, at 7 o'clock saw much smoke of Whitehaven.

A few desultory cannon shots from the guns left unspiked and those on board a handful of ships in the harbour were fired in the direction of the retreating boats.

As Jones recalls later in the memoirs he wrote in order to prove to the authorities what a brave and daring man he had been and that they owed him a great deal of prize money:

... the fires spread and rose to a great height...I could no longer postpone my retreat. I made it in very good order. When all of my force was embarked I remained on the far breakwater to contemplate at length the terror, panic and stupidity of the inhabitants, who numbered no less than 10,000 and stood as still as statues or scurried senselessly here and there to gain some high ground beyond the city.

Whether Jones's retreat was as clever and orderly as he suggests is uncertain. What is sure is that the population of Whitehaven was unlikely to have been greater than 9,000, that the panic occurred later when it had been established what had taken place and that Whitehaven was not then and is not now a city.

This is perhaps nit-picking, but it puts into perspective some of the idealistic notions that have always coloured the Whitehaven Raid - notions that were spread by Jones himself in his memoirs.

So, what was the damage? Again, according to Jones, there were 'approximately 400 foreign and domestic merchantmen, averaging 250-tons burden each' in the harbour. In fact the fire affected only one boat, the collier *Thompson* and was, according to the *Cumberland Magazine*, 'speedily extinguished, without damaging any other vessel'. The boat was back in service within weeks.

In military or naval terms, the raid was ineffectual in the extreme. Whitehaven is not in a great strategic position. Even nowadays, with a modern road network, it is remote from much of the rest of mainland Britain. At the end of the eighteenth century, its communication with the rest of the country was largely through the boats in the harbour.

In psychological terms, however, it was a different story. There is no doubt that this raid sent shivers down the spines of those who lived along the western coast of Northern England and Scotland. The ports and harbours were of no military significance, but in an era long before the word 'propaganda' had been invented, the raid on Whitehaven had the effect of sowing the seeds of fear amongst coastal dwellers.

Indeed, given the very remoteness of Whitehaven, the fact that details of the raid were so widely, and so quickly reported – *Lloyd's Evening Post* of London reported the event within a week – indicates the extent of the panic.

According to Mrs Reginald de Koven, in her extensive work of 1930, the raid 'cast the whole island into unreasoning and hysterical panic' and led directly to the creation of a volunteer force. In Whitehaven itself, a public subscription raised the enormous sum of £850.

To improve the town's defences, local militia were marched at some speed from inland and a curfew was imposed. Insurance rates for merchant vessels also doubled.

Some writers have also made great mention of the importance of the date – 23 April, St George's Day. Unlike many other people, however, the English have never tended to celebrate their national Saint's day. Also, Jones had been blown off-course a few days earlier and had intended going ashore elsewhere. So, it is probably best to view the timing and place of the raid and the fact that he chose Whitehaven as a mixture of happenstance, luck, the weather and the tides.

To Jones's supporters, the Whitehaven raid has always been seen as an act of daring and heroism. It may not be the most important item on the Jones résumé, but it always features amongst his most audacious adventures and is certainly an important aspect of the chapbook mythology that sprung up around the Scottish sailor. To his detractors, and especially to the eighteenth century English, it was seen as the cowardly act of a traitorous pirate.

As with all such matters, the truth lies somewhere between the two. It is interesting, however, to see the picture of Jones that the whole process of the raid reveals. If Jones intended it to be a propaganda coup, it certainly had the desired effect. However, I suspect that if that were the case, then it was more to do with Jones's standing than it was to do with genuine support for an independent America.

In fact, the raid on Whitehaven took place against a backdrop of insubordination, even possible mutiny. When the idea of the raid was mooted, the ship's surgeon, Ezra Green again records that he was not happy with the idea and declared that 'nothing could be got ... by burning poor people's property'. Jones himself further records that his two lieutenants (Elijah Hale and Thomas Simpson) were 'not demonstrating the high spirits this enterprise required ... declared they were ill with fatigue'.

This was not the first time that Jones would have difficulty managing his men, nor would it be the last. His immense courage and daring was never matched by any skill in dealing with people, least of all those under his command. His inability to exert authority and control over the men in his service is a recurrent theme of his career. He is often held responsible for two deaths – one in which he ran his sword through the ringleader of a crew that was becoming, unsurprisingly, mutinous, because they wanted pay and shore leave when he commanded a merchant vessel, *The Betsy*. The other was when he had his ship's carpenter, Mungo Maxwell, flogged - a common enough punishment in those days. However, when the carpenter didn't appear sufficiently chastened, Jones set about him with a belaying pin. Not long after, Maxwell died from yellow fever and, although Jones was exonerated of murder, the smell of the incident haunted him for years. Indeed, he disappeared under the historical radar for a few years and when he re-emerged he began to call himself a variety of names, eventually setting on John Paul Jones.

It is scarcely surprising that the crew of *The Ranger* should not want to follow Jones on his enterprise. He had already miscalculated the distance between *Ranger* and the shore. Instead of the raiding party arriving near midnight, it took them the best part of three hours, rowing against the tide to reach the beach next to the harbour.

According to some accounts, Lieutenant Edward Meier (sometimes spelled Meyer) had to be left behind with the boats at the shore to ensure that no-one rowed away without their captain. Whether this is true or not is hard to tell, but it does indicate something of the level of unease amongst his men. This reluctance of his men to carry out his orders ensured that from a military point of view, the Whitehaven Raid was a damp squib.

It's generally held to be true that freedom fighters are terrorists who happen to end up on the winning side. When Jones died, *The Cumberland Pacquet* of 31 July 1792 carried an obituary notice. Unsurprisingly, it is not the most glowing testimony that he would receive, but it certainly reflected the feelings of many of the residents of Cumberland, and especially those of Whitehaven, who had felt for years that he had betrayed them. With the death of John Paul Jones, 'in great indigence ... thus has ended the career of a man who made much noise in the world, and did some mischief...the insidious attempt to burn the shipping of Whitehaven ... will long be remembered ... Where was the heroism of fiercely attacking an unguarded place, avowedly not for the purpose of plunder, but for the sake of

The villain turns hero – John Paul Jones now even has a pub named after him.

involving its inhabitants in ruin? No tribute of approbation could possibly be bestowed on such an act, but by persons of congenial spirit.'

Time, of course, lends enchantment. There are now several tributes to Jones in the area. Present day Whitehaven is now proud of its links. A pub near the harbour bears his name and from time to time, historical re-enactments of the raid are staged as a kind of open-air theatre and the official pardon of John Paul Jones, in 1998, was a well-attended piece of pageantry.

History would be as tidy as a Hollywood film if we could find some reference to an event that would trigger in the young John Paul some dislike or even hatred of the town. In that way, we could ascribe to it the reason behind his attack on the harbour some seventeen years later. However, there seems to be no discernible reason why he should have taken against the town. In the film made of his life, an uninspiring hagiography in which he even throws the cat-o-nine tails out of the window declaring that he'll have none of that aboard his ship, a young Paul Jones watches as vicious English redcoats mercilessly suppress the wearing of tartan. True, tartan-wearing was suppressed, but the Scottish side of the Solway Firth has never been noted for the wearing of the kilt!

Jones was a clever sailor, but also an opportunist and a martinet. He could see no other viewpoint but his own and anyone who disagreed with him immediately became his enemy. If we're able to diagnose retrospectively that Leonardo da Vinci, for instance, was probably dyslexic, then we could say that Jones had Narcissistic Personality Disorder. He was also capable of the most outrageous pandering to those in higher social positions when he wanted to ingratiate himself with them. In the dedication of his memoirs to King Louis XVI of France, he pens this appalling piece of doggerel:

> *Protector of fair Freedoms Rights,*
> *Louis, thy Virtues suit a God!*
> *The good Man in thy praise delights,*
> *And Tyrants trimble at thy nod!*

> *The people's Father, lov'd so well,*
> *May time respect! – when thou art gone,*
> *May each new-year of hist'ry tell,*
> *Thy sons, with lustre fill thy Throne.*

Even if he'd never set fire to a coal-boat or been responsible for the deaths of several men, just writing that would be foul deed enough.

Chapter 2

Forced Marriage
and False Imprisonment
1788

He had obviously been Ann Heslop's target for some time. Not for her some toyboy, or even someone close in age to her – someone in their forties, perhaps, with a good, steady job labouring in the fields. No, it had to be Jonathan Sewell.

Jonathan Sewell had two things going in his favour. The first was that he owned some land from which he received an annual income of around £100 per year – approximately equivalent to £80,000 when compared with average annual earnings today. The second was that he was, according to a court report, 'a weak, infirm man, upwards of 70 years of age … much addicted to liquor … subject to get drunk and thereby rendered incapable of taking care of himself'.

So, Ann Heslop hatched a plan to make the most of the elderly chap's wealth and weaknesses. Her first attempt at getting her hands on his cash ended in failure. In May 1788, she and a man called David Wilson, who died before the case came to court, took Jonathan Sewell out on a drinking session around the inns of Carlisle. When he was totally incapable, they ladled him into a carriage and whisked him over the Scottish border to Gretna Green, where the laws on marriage famously allowed for a quicker union than they did in England. Luckily for Jonathan Sewell, whoever was due to officiate at the ceremony was not totally happy and refused to carry out the service.

She tried again, but her second attempt was also doomed to failure. They had obviously slept on the plan for a while, working on a few details, although the broad brush strokes remained the same. This time, on 3 July 1788, they got Jonathan Sewell drunk and bundled him into a chaise, but instead of taking him to Gretna, took him to Edinburgh. She was accompanied on this excursion by a certain John Irving. Poor old Jonathan Sewell tried to escape from the chaise as it rattled along, but although he broke several windows, his captors managed to pacify him with his good friend, the bottle of spirituous liquors.

Luckily, Sewell had some good friends and his brother-in-law Joseph Graham, his cousin John Bond, his solicitor Richard Lowthian and a Mr John Mitchison chased off after him. The rescue party found Ann Heslop and Jonathan Sewell at the Crook Inn on the road between Moffat and Edinburgh in the early hours of the morning of 6 July.

When the rescue party caught up with them, Jonathan Sewell and Ann Heslop were in bed together. Given that Ann Heslop managed to hold him down in the bed with just an arm, he was so drunk that one suspects that nothing had gone on between the two of them. She produced a certificate of marriage that stated that she and Jonathan Sewell were married. Not only was the rescue party disturbing the honeymoon, but the paperwork proved that the couple had been in Scotland for at least six weeks and that the banns had been read out on three occasions. It was clearly a forgery. His rescue party managed to get him back to Cumberland and to fight off the intentions of Ann Heslop and her cronies for a while.

One would have thought that if this excitement didn't kill the old boy, the least it might do would be to warn him off drinking with Ann Heslop. But no! On 13 September of the same year, whilst Jonathan Sewell was cutting corn at Durdar, Ann Heslop, with Thomas Wallis and David Wilson, two yeomen from Penrith, joined him in the field and encouraged him to drink 'large quantities of ale and spirituous liquors', whilst yet another post chaise stood by, waiting to cart him off again.

This time they'd altered the plan again and took him to Thomas Wallis's house in Penrith, the next day moving him to Hood-Foot, where he spent another three days, after which he was moved over the mountains to Stanhope in Weardale, County Durham, where he was imprisoned in the house of John Walton. His captors kept him there for a fortnight until the fuss had died down, then brought him back to Penrith, where they kept him imprisoned in the garret of Thomas Wallis's house for an incredible thirty-six weeks.

His friends soon realised where he was and three weeks into his imprisonment, they applied for a writ of *habeas corpus*. This was served against David Wilson, his brother Thomas Leeke Wilson, who was a butcher in Penrith, and Thomas Wallis. They disobeyed this writ, so it is hardly surprising that they were met by the full might of the law.

Ann Heslop, her brother John Boustead, Thomas and John Wilson, and Thomas Wallis appeared before the Court of *Nisi Prius* in Carlisle on 15 August 1789, a year after their first aborted attempt to abduct Jonathan Sewell. There were numerous charges. Amongst other things, they were accused of:

> ... *wickedly and maliciously devising and intending to defraud, aggrieve, and injure Jonathan Sewell, an honest and liege subject of this realm, wrongfully, wickedly and maliciously with force and arms, did amongst themselves conspire, consult and agree together wrongfully, injuriously and unjustly to force the said Jonathan Sewell to marry (he, the said Jonathan Sewell, being an unmarried person) and to take to wife the said Ann Heslop ...*

... the charge sheet ran on, overflowing with words that seem to mean more or less the same thing, but nonetheless, the defendants were also charged that:

> ... *with force and arms did beat, bruise, and otherwise ill-treat the said Jonathan Sewell; and forced and obliged him to suffer and undergo great inclemency and severity of weather, and great labour, hardships, and fatigue of body in travelling about in diverse parts of this realm by day and night, and during that time, also in further pursuance of the said unlawful and wicked conspiracy, consultation, and agreement ... wickedly and maliciously terrified the said Jonathan Sewell with diverse menaces and threats of further bodily injury to the said Jonathan Sewell and of loss of his life, to wit.*

There were also eight other counts to be answered, but happily our chronicler did not go into any further detail.

The court case was a mixed bag of damning evidence from the prosecution witnesses and flimsy ripostes from the defence. One senses that there was plenty of money on offer for those who would paint the right picture. A servant to Thomas Wallis, Elizabeth Gristlethwaite, went on record as saying that in his time at Thomas Wallis's house, Jonathan Sewell could be seen in several rooms – and was thus not held prisoner against his own will, but also stated that she never saw him drunk, which seems entirely unlikely.

Several of the defendants had been sucked into the affair with promises of money at the end. It would seem that Thomas Wallis was after land. Whether Ann Heslop was merely a lure for the ageing drunkard Sewell, or if she was the ringleader of a little gang who could then make her comfortable for the rest of her life, is hard to say. What is stated in several places is that Ann Heslop was a middle-aged prostitute.

According to Jonathan Sewell's solicitor, Richard Lowthian, Ann Heslop told him that she had been in love with Jonathan Sewell for many years, whilst it would seem that Jonathan Sewell 'never had any inclination to be married, even when younger'. Even Jonathan Sewell himself went on record at the later trial to say of his 'bride': 'I would rather have gone twelve miles about than have gone into the town where she lived. I never in all my life had carnal dealings with her, or any other woman!'

The Wilsons were sentenced to a year's imprisonment, Thomas Wallis to two years and Ann Heslop was sentenced to three years in Newgate Gaol. Whilst several of her co-defendants fled into Scotland to evade their sentence; Ann was actually sent to Newgate, a place from which she would never emerge.

It is unlikely that Ann Heslop saw much beyond the £100 a year that would (at best) have been her widow's pension. The marriage certificate was almost definitely a forgery. However, when she died in Newgate Gaol just two years after she had become Jonathan Sewell's serial abductress, *The Times* referred to her as Ann Sewell and believed that she had '... undergone a variety of cruel persecution and imprisonment for her marriage with Mr Jonathan Sewell'. It is difficult to tell why *The Thunderer* should have thought that, given the weight of evidence against Ann Heslop and her co-conspirators. However, it is likely that Ann was just an organ-grinder to Thomas Wallis's monkey, the lure of owning yet more land in the Penrith area being just too much for him.

Chapter 3

The Keswick Imposter
1802

I n July 1802, the tongues of the great and the good of Keswick were wagging. The arrival of the Honourable Colonel Alexander Augustus Hope, Member of Parliament for Linlithgow and brother of the Earl of Hopetoun meant that there would be a man of rank and importance in the town for the remainder of the summer.

Colonel Hope MP arrived in a splendid carriage and immediately put up at the *Queen's Head* in Keswick. True, it was unusual for a man of such importance to travel without at least a man-servant and his speech was perhaps a little less grammatical than one might expect (was it the latest London small-talk?), but his visiting cards were impressive and, according to the *Newgate Calendar*, 'His face was handsome, his person genteel, his eyes blue, and his complexion fair.' Besides, the post that arrived regularly was addressed to him in that name. Who were the people of Keswick to question him too closely?

Colonel Hope was a fascinating man. Soon the other visitors of import were regaled with his stories, which even if they might have been a little boastful, were always witty and colourful. He talked of his estates in Derbyshire and Cheshire. Tales of his exploits in Egypt, Turkey and Italy, where he fought several duels made fascinating listening. So too did his adventures in the American War. These explained his slight limp, his injured fingers and the scar on his face. This was a man who could trace his ancestors back to the Plantagenets, which he often did, as well as quoting from the scriptures.

Another short-term resident of Keswick was a certain Nathaniel More, whose niece (although she is variously reported as his daughter or sister), Sarah, had accompanied him on his journey to

The Fish Hotel *– formerly the* Fish Inn *and home to Mary Robinson, the Beauty of Buttermere, whom John Hatfield bigamously married.*

Keswick. She was soon under the spell of the charming Colonel Hope. Such was the impression that the Colonel made that he had soon persuaded More that his niece should marry him and preparations began for the forthcoming wedding.

Whilst Sarah More was sorting her trousseau, Colonel Hope went to Buttermere to do a spot of fishing. Here, at the *Fish Inn*, he encountered the young woman often called the Beauty of Buttermere. Mary Robinson had been something of a tourist attraction in the Lake District for some time. Joseph Budworth's 1792 guidebook, *A Fortnight's Ramble to the Lakes*, concentrates mainly on descriptions of the landscapes. However, he turned his pen to Mary Robinson with a description that was to make her name:

> *Her hair was thick and long, of a dark brown, and though unadorned with ringlets, did not seem to want them; her face was a fine contour, with full eyes, and lips as red as vermilion; her cheeks had more of the lily than the rose; and although she had never been out of the village … she had a manner about her which seemed better calculated to set off dress, than dress her. She was a very Lavinia, 'Seeming when unadorn'd, adorn'd the most.'*

Colonel Hope was smitten and soon was proposing marriage to the beautiful Mary as well. To begin with, she rebuffed him. His idea of eloping to be married in Scotland seemed out of the question because they had not known each other long enough and, besides, there was the difference in rank. She was an innkeeper's daughter (even if her father was reasonably wealthy by local standards) and he was the Honourable Alexander Augustus Hope. But our Colonel was persistent. He worked on both Mary and her father until they consented. He and Mary were married at Lorton Church, near Cockermouth, on 2 October 1802.

Lorton Church – Mary Robinson married John Hatfield (under his assumed identity) here in October 1802. Reports of the marriage were to lead to Hatfield's exposure.

Whilst the news of the event shocked the More family, it stunned the real Colonel Hope's family. Samuel Taylor Coleridge, whilst visiting his friend William Wordsworth, picked up the story of the marriage of the Beauty of Buttermere and wrote a piece on the subject of her marriage for the *Morning Post*. The real Colonel Hope's family thought he was in Vienna and when they managed to confirm that this was indeed the case, then the Colonel Hope on holiday in the Lake District soon began to lose credibility.

This was compounded when a Welsh judge, Mr Harding, passed through Keswick. He knew the real Colonel Hope and was perplexed when introduced to the Keswick version. The unravelling continued, when the Judge insisted that 'Hope' be questioned closely about his personal details. Contradictions emerged in the Colonel's story and he was placed under the supervision of a local constable. However, the constable was not too worried that his charge might escape and let the Honourable Alexander Augustus Hope go on a little fishing expedition on Derwentwater.

Hatfield seized his chance and fled Keswick for the coast, absconding to Ravenglass. Nowadays, Ravenglass is considered to be one of the prettiest places in Cumbria. It's the only coastal village within the Lake District National Park and with its main street of snaggled fisherman's cottages, is often photographed for colourful calendars. Richard Ayton, an early travel writer, writing in 1826 describes the village in rather less flattering terms:

At the north end of the Esk Meals there is an opening in the sand hills about a quarter of a mile broad, through which three rivers, the Esk, the Mite, and the Irt, discharge themselves in one stream into the sea. At high water the sea on its confluence with these rivers spreads over a wide space within the sand-hills, which on the retiring of the tide is left, except in the channels of the rivers, a dreary extent of sand, mud, and marsh. On the border of this dismal water stands Ravenglass, a dirty, ragged, forlorn looking town, which, considered in all its relations, in its own miserable place, with the title of a town, in the kingdom. There is no trade of any kind in it, the people picking up a scanty subsistence by fishing, which in the summer season they help out by labouring at the harvest. We had seen and were to see nothing so mournfully bad as Ravenglass...

The natural harbour at Ravenglass – John Hatfield hid here for several days after escaping from Keswick.

If that's how it was in 1826, one hesitates to think how it must have been just twenty-odd years earlier. But it was from here, that Hatfield bribed a fisherman to take him to Ulverston and from Ulverston, Hatfield then slipped off back to his homeland of Cheshire.

The Times of 23 October 1802 carried the report of his doings under the title 'Fraudulent Marriage' and the whole country knew that the poor Beauty of Buttermere had been duped. It was a scandal of huge proportions and public sympathy was on her side.

By now it was patently obvious that the man calling himself Colonel, the Honourable Alexander Augustus Hope, Member of Parliament for Linlithgow and brother of the Earl of Hopetoun was

The Queen's Hotel – *formerly the* Queen's Inn – *where John Hatfield stayed whilst masquerading as the Colonel the Honourable Alexander Augustus Hope.*

not who he said he was. In fact, he was a draper's assistant from Cheshire called John Hatfield, who had committed a string of frauds and deceptions before arriving in Keswick on his latest adventure.

Meanwhile, whilst Hatfield was attempting to evade arrest, his carriage at the *Queen's Head* in Keswick was searched and amongst his possessions was an elaborate dressing-case. On close inspection, the case was found to have a false bottom and in it were several letters that revealed more about his real life.

He had long had a habit of wooing women and either marrying them or otherwise defrauding them of dowries or other money.

During his time in Keswick and the surrounding area, Hatfield seems to have promised marriage to at least four women. Along with Miss More, whose marriage preparations seem to have been well under way, there was also a maidservant at the *Queen's Head*, the daughter of the Mr Burkitt with whom he went on his fishing expeditions. However, he seems to have been particularly keen on Mary.

As a young man working in the linen trade in Cheshire, a local farmer had disclosed to him that the girl he was bringing up as his own, was in fact the daughter of Lord Robert Manners, who would settle a thousand pounds on her at marriage. He inveigled himself into marriage with her, and once he had the cash in his pocket, bought himself a phaeton and set off to London, where he soon exhausted the money and then began to rack up debts.

Hatfield had at least one other wife, living in Devon. Amongst his many misdeeds, he had been gaoled in Scarborough in 1793 for debt and this lady had become smitten with him and when he heard that she had money, he too soon became enamoured. According to reports, when Hatfield left on his jaunt to Keswick, she had already had one child by him and another was on the way.

Later, Hatfield had attempted to run for Parliament in Queenborough in Devon, but he again racked up so many bad debts that he and a clergyman who'd haplessly cashed dud cheques for him were forced to flee. Meanwhile, the authorities were desperate to catch Hatfield and they circulated a detailed description of him:

Notorious Impostor, swindler and felon! John Hatfield, who lately married a young woman, commonly called the Beauty of Buttermere, under an assumed name: height about five feet ten inches; aged about forty-four; full face, bright eyes, thick eyebrows, strong but light beard, good complexion, with some colour; thick, but not very prominent nose, smiling countenance, fine teeth, a scar on one of his cheeks near the chin, very long thick light hair, and a great deal of it grey, done up in a club; stiff, square shouldered, full breast and chest, rather corpulent, and strong limbed, but very active; and has rather a spring in his gait, with apparently a little hitch in bringing up one leg; the two middle fingers of his left hand are stiff

from an old wound: he has something of the Irish brogue in his speech;
fluent and elegant in his language, great command of words,
frequently puts his hand to his heart; very fond of compliments, and
generally addressing himself to persons most distinguished by rank or
situation, attentive in the extreme to females, and likely to insinuate
himself where there are young ladies.

It also went on to describe the various exploits of which he was likely
to boast. Surprisingly, although there were probably plenty of people
who would have known him in his own county of Cheshire and the
Bow Street Runners were after him, it was not until Hatfield reached
Brecon in Wales that he was arrested. Even here, he wouldn't give his
real name, insisting that he was called John Henry or Tudor Henry,
until he was identified as Hatfield and returned to Cumbria for trial.

At the Assizes, he faced two charges of what essentially amounted
to forgery or attempting to obtain money under false pretences and
the crime for which he was to hang. Whilst the bigamy might have
gained him notoriety, there were far more serious charges to be
faced. In passing himself off as a Member of Parliament, he had
used the postal service to send letters free of charge and this was a
capital offence.

According to *The Newgate Calendar*:

On the day of his execution, the 3rd of September, 1803, the sheriffs,
the bailiffs, and the Carlisle volunteer cavalry attended at the jail
door about half-past three, together with a post-chaise and a hearse.
A prodigious crowd had assembled. It was market-day, and people
had come from a distance of many miles out of mere curiosity.
Hatfield, when he left the prison, wished all his fellow-prisoners to be
happy. He then took farewell of the clergyman, who attended him to
the door of the chaise, and mounted the steps with much steadiness
and composure. The jailer and the executioner went along with him.
The latter had been brought from Dumfries upon a retaining fee of ten
guineas.

It was exactly four o'clock when the procession moved from the jail,
passing through the Scotch Gate, in about twelve minutes it arrived
at the sands. Half the yeomanry went before the carriage, and the
other half behind. Upon their arrival on the ground they formed a
ring round the scaffold. .

As soon as the carriage door was opened by the under-sheriff the culprit alighted with his two companions. A small dung-cart, boarded over, had been placed under the gibbet. A ladder was placed to this stage, which he instantly ascended. He immediately untied his neck-handkerchief and placed a bandage over his eyes. Then he desired the hangman, who was extremely awkward, to be as expert as possible about it, and that he would wave a handkerchief when he was ready. The hangman not having fixed the rope in its proper place, he put up his hand and turned it himself. He also tied his cap, took his handkerchief from his own neck, and tied it about his head also. Then he requested the jailer to step upon the platform and pinion his arms a little harder, saying that when he had lost his senses he might attempt to place them to his neck. The rope was completely fixed about five minutes before four o'clock; it was slack, and he merely said: 'May the Almighty bless you all.' Nor did he falter in the least when he tied the cap, shifted the rope, and took his handkerchief from his neck.

Great apprehensions were entertained that it would be necessary to tie him up a second time. The noose slipped twice and he fell down about eighteen inches. At last his feet almost touched the ground, but his excessive weight, which occasioned this accident, speedily relieved him from pain. He expired in a moment, and without any struggle.

That was the end of Hatfield. As for Mary Robinson, she married a local farmer, Richard Harrison a few years later, had four children and lead a contented life in Cumberland, before dying in 1834.

The story of John Hatfield and the Beauty of Buttermere has been the inspiration for many writers. Melvyn Bragg's book *The Maid of Buttermere* is a fictionalised account of the story. Even Wordsworth was moved to write the following lines:

I mean, O distant Friend! a story drawn
From our own ground, the Maid of Buttermere,
And how, unfaithful to a virtuous wife
Deserted and deceived, the Spoiler came
And wooed the artless daughter of the hills,
And wedded her, in cruel mockery
Of love and marriage bonds. These words to thee
Must needs bring back the moment when we first,

Ere the broad world rang with the maiden's name,
Beheld her serving at the cottage inn;
Both stricken, as she entered or withdrew,
With admiration of her modest mien
And carriage, marked by unexampled grace.
We since that time not unfamiliarly
Have seen her, - her discretion have observed,
Her just opinions, delicate reserve,
Her patience, and humility of mind
Unspoiled by commendation and the excess
Of public notice - an offensive light
To a meek spirit suffering inwardly.
From this memorial tribute to my theme
I was returning, when, with sundry forms
Commingled-shapes which met me in the way
That we must tread - thy image rose again,
Maiden of Buttermere! She lives in peace
Upon the spot where she was born and reared;

His fellow poet, Samuel Taylor Coleridge, who had followed the story for the *Morning Post,* wrote of Mary Robinson: 'It seems that there are some circumstances attending her birth and true parentage, which would account for her striking superiority in mind and manners, in a way extremely flattering to the prejudices of rank and birth.' He never explained what he meant by that. But perhaps Mary herself was, even if unwittingly, an impostor too.

Chapter 4

Charles Samuel Cave, the Swindler
1824

Mr Cave was not at all well when he checked into the *King's Arms* in Carlisle on 25 February 1824. He had come north for the sake of his health, and he now had 'a dangerous pain in the heart'. The coach ride had been extremely hard work for he had come a long way to be there. As the other residents were soon to find out, he lived at Thorney Abbey, the seat of his paternal ancestors, in Cambridgeshire, where he had extensive property. He was tired from the long journey.

For the next few days his health improved enough for him to enquire as to the reliability of a firm of bankers called Forster whom he believed did business in Carlisle, and to make the acquaintance of the innkeeper's sister-in-law, a Miss Mary Cape. She was a pretty young woman, not quite yet of age, but who would inherit an income of £900 a year when the time came (worth as much as £60,000 in today's money).

Despite Miss Cape's charming presence, poor Mr Cave's recovery was short-lived. He had a pain in his chest whilst in church, then not a fortnight after his arrival, he was taken badly in the street. Forced to return to his hotel room, he realised that with his health in its current parlous state a man with all his wealth and property really must make a will.

On advice from the innkeeper, Mr Donald, Charles Samuel Cave sent for a local solicitor, Mr George Saul, who had an excellent reputation. George Saul arrived as soon as he could and Charles Samuel Cave began to dictate his will. He named James Biffin of Chichester, merchant, and James Farnell, of the same place, builder, as trustees and he told them to deal with all his real estate in or near Chichester, and at Horsley Down,

... consisting of freehold dwelling houses and closes of land, in the occupation of William Artou and others, as tenants. Also at Whittlesey in Cambridgeshire, in the Isle of Ely ... a house and four acres of land, copyhold, in the occupation of Thomas Cave, his brother and £6,000 in the Funds new four per Cents.

Furthermore, the gentlemen were to receive all rents and interest and pay them to his mother until her death, except for £500 which they were to give to Joseph Scrimshaw, natural son of his brother and for whom he stood as godfather. He also included £100 to his godson for an apprenticeship or trade he may think proper to go to. After his mother's death they were to sell everything off and divide the proceeds between his brothers and sisters in equal shares. If they were dead, this money was to go to their wives and husbands and if they were dead to their children. He also wanted to be buried at his beloved Thorney Abbey.

There were several witnesses to Mr Cave's will, including Miss Cape's brother-in-law (Mr Donald, the innkeeper) and Mr Scott, who was Miss Cape's guardian until she came of age. As a man of wealth, property and position, it was important that Mr Cave be able to trust those who had come to witness his last will and testament.

Happily, although Mr Cave had feared for the worst, the next day he felt extraordinarily well and was back on his feet again. He called round on his new solicitor, Mr Saul, and wondered if perhaps the will he had just made was useless as he was about to be married. This information was strictly confidential. Mr Saul must discuss it with no-one as he needed to decide on a settlement for his bride-to-be.

He also wanted some advice from Mr Saul. A certain Mr Norman had approached him. He was hoping that Charles Samuel Cave might be willing to advance him a mortgage of £2,400 against a property. Would Mr Saul go and look at the property on his behalf, as he was 'acting with safety ... for he was excessively cautious in all his money transactions?' Meanwhile, he wanted Mr Saul to arrange for a sum of money to be advanced to him. In Wisbech, in Cambridgeshire, there was a gentleman called Peckover, who was a trustee of the estate left in trust to Charles

Samuel Cave by his late father, God rest his soul. Cave asked the solicitor to write to Mr Peckover to arrange to have the sum of £2,400 released from the £6,000 worth of shares that were held in the trust. If the property looked good for a mortgage, then Mr Saul could arrange for the money to go straight to Mr Norman.

Cave left, but was soon back in Mr Saul's offices. He had a new scheme. He had heard that Coledale Hall was to be disposed of and perhaps it might be a wiser investment for him to buy that, as rumour had it that the Hall might be going for a very good price. He asked his solicitor to postpone asking Mr Peckover for money, then made an offer in writing of £1,850 to Mrs Sissons of Appleby for Coledale Hall. After all, as he was trying to think through where best to buy, he was not sure exactly how much money he would need, so it would be best to delay cashing in shares for the time being.

Meanwhile, Charles Samuel Cave had not failed to notice the allure of the innkeeper's sister-in-law, Miss Mary Cape. In early March, just a short while after he had arrived in Carlisle, he proposed marriage to the fair Mary Cape and she accepted, although she was fully aware that her guardian, Mr Scott, and her brother-in-law, Mr Donald might not appreciate the haste of it all. She was in no hurry to marry, but he was. He settled on her a property he owned in Sussex – that would put her mind to rest and fan the flames of her ardour.

On 10 March 1824, the circus was in town and a whole party descended to enjoy the fun. It was the perfect cover for the young lovebirds. Charles Samuel Cave and Mary Cape saw this as their opportunity to slip away. They took a carriage the ten miles needed to cross the Scottish border to Gretna Green, where they could be married without the delays typical in England. But Mr Donald got wind of the plan and when he realised the couple was missing, he followed in hot pursuit. However, when he arrived in Gretna Green, Charles Samuel Cave told him that he was too late to stop the marriage. This wasn't true, and whilst Mr Donald was in one room, the couple slipped into another and were then married.

The family was rather disappointed about the affair but, seeing that Charles Samuel Cave and Mary were living as man and wife, they decided that there should be a second wedding, this time in England. Charles Samuel Cave was a little reluctant about this, but eventually he was persuaded that it was for the best. On 25 March, Mr and Mrs Cave tied the knot again in St Cuthbert's church in Carlisle.

Of course Mary couldn't know – and it might have made her a little more hesitant to rush into marriage, and possibly a lot more hesitant to sign over the bulk of her inheritance to her new husband, but Mary Cape was Charles Samuel Cave's fourth wife. Perhaps she could have coped with that, but unfortunately for Mary, only one of his previous brides had shuffled off this mortal coil.

His first wife, a woman by the name of Mary Nicholls, had died, leaving him with two children, at which point he had married a Sarah Kent, then in July 1820 a lady called Charlotte Bingham, whom he had then deserted just before their child was born. Furthermore, rather than being the heir to a fortune in Thorney Abbey, Charles Samuel Cave was a barrel-maker, an artisan cooper who had spent the last few years hopping around the country moving from one act of fraud to the next.

Of course, none of the trusting people of Carlisle realised this. Not least the solicitor Mr Saul, who had advanced Charles Samuel Cave around £40, whilst he made up his mind what to do. For the time being, Charles Samuel Cave lived on Mr Saul's loan and what money he could prise from his wife's eventual estate.

Meanwhile, Cave needed to keep up appearances. The reply had come from Mrs Sissons. She was unwilling to sell Coledale Hall for less than 2,000 guineas. If Mr Cave were to have the Hall for himself and his young bride, then he would have to ask Mr Peckover for almost the original total of £2,400.

Charles Samuel Cave must have realised he was on borrowed time. He ascertained from George Saul that if he were to write to Mr Peckover, they could not expect a reply until at least 31 March. He authorised Mr Saul to write, presumably because he had run out of ideas on how to forestall him. Cave then organised to go to Appleby on 29 March, ostensibly to see friends and meet with bankers, but must have been preparing either some back-up plan or simply to have disappeared to the next town where he could find people trusting – or gullible – enough to support his lifestyle.

The letter from Mr Peckover arrived earlier than expected. On 28 March, Mr George Saul received his reply. According to the *Carlisle Patriot*, Peckover's letter stated that he knew nothing of any such person as Charles Samuel Cave:

> *There was a Samuel Cave resident in this place a short time ago, who took a gentleman in named Cox for several hundred pounds, and decamped and has not since been heard of – and, I understand, left a wife to bewail his absence.*

Mr Saul had finally tumbled to the ruse. Cave had obtained money from him under false pretences. He sent for the authorities and Cave was apprehended and taken to Carlisle Gaol. It was only as Mr Saul began to look into Cave's background that he found that as well as being a swindler, Charles Samuel Cave was partial to a bit of polygamy, finding new twists to the story with every reply he received from his enquiries.

He left few stones unturned, digging out references to Cave's behaviour from Sussex and Cambridgeshire. From a law firm in Wisbech, Mr Saul ascertained that:

> *We find by the parish Register that Samuel Cave was married to Charlotte Bingham, spinster, on the 3rd July 1820, and on comparing the hand-writing contained in your letter with the writing in the parish Register, there is no doubt of their being the same, with the addition of Charles in your letter. We also find, that in consequence of some disputes between Cave and his wife, she left him and went to reside at a village in Peterborough with her mother, where she was confined, we have not as yet been able to ascertain the name of the village but have put the matter in train to obtain that information. Samuel Cave is well know to Mr ------, who attended him several times relative to a fraudulent transaction on the part of Cave with the late Mr Thomas Cox, of this place, who advanced him a large sum of money when he was a cooper in this town, and which he was never repaid.*

A butcher in Chichester wrote telling him:

> *A person calling himself Chas. Cave, in every respect answering the description in your letter, left Chichester about the 20th of Feb. last*

after swindling me and all my neighbours. He came here in April 1823 as a journeyman cooper, and worked for a Mr Biffin, a respectable cooper and timber merchant of this city, nearly up to Christmas last, about which time Messrs Hiard and Cutten, coach makers, wished to dissolve partnership and it was agreed that Cutten should have the business when Cave, who lived in part of Cutten's house, agreed to lend him £1,100 for 7 years, which sum he said he had ready, as, he asserted, he had a considerable property and a little before the business was to be settled he borrowed of Cutten at different times £60. While this was going on, he agreed to purchase some houses and building ground of a Mr Arton. Attorneys were employed, building materials bought, his own house furnished, a treat given to his acquaintances, when I had the honour to supply meat for the table to the amount of £1 6d, for which I was never paid. However, a day was fixed when the houses were to be paid for, and the money lent to Cutten: on the Sunday before, he borrowed £20 of a Mr Carter, a builder, whom he had employed to build his houses, and then disappeared: and as far as I can learn, cheated the people here to the amount of £250-£300, besides expense of writings etc. He left his wife behind, who was taken away by her father, Mr John Natley, malter of Uphurstbourne, nr Andover, Hants: she was a widow, in business as a cooper at Whitchurch, in that county, where Cave went to work as a journeyman. He there married her, representing himself as having property – failed in business and came to Chichester for work. Before he lived with a Mrs Kent, he worked in Basingstoke, Hants. He is a native of Thorney, Cambridgeshire, where his mother lives with a Mr Watson of Thorney Abbey. He has been married before he married Mrs Kent, and said his wife was dead: he had a child or two by his first wife – one was left at Chichester by his wife when he ran away, and has since been sent for by Mrs Cave etc.

The charge against Charles Samuel Cave was now far more serious – that of bigamy. He would appear before the Summer Assizes in Carlisle in August of that year. Meanwhile, he could stay in Carlisle Gaol where his chances of marrying yet more young ladies of good fortune were low.

Of course, the case caused a sensation. It had everything going for it – a hoodwinked solicitor, a trail of debts, deceit and broken hearts that ran the length of the country, and not least a young girl whose reputation had been besmirched.

The newspapers really couldn't make their mind up about Charles Samuel Cave. Not least about the way he looked. The *Carlisle Patriot* described him with more than a hint of underlying snobbery as '...a rather good looking man, resembling a superior kind of horse-dealer in appearance'. Later, they changed their minds and Charles Samuel Cave became rather less prepossessing – 'not withstanding a rather inanimate physiognomy, a not very engaging address, and a most palpable ignorance so far as education goes, the adventurer managed matters with the ingenuity highly expressive of his natural talent for mystification'. Money can make up for a lack of good looks, even when it's imaginary money. For of course, the whole of Charles Samuel Cave's life was one huge fabrication. He had managed to dupe a lot of people, many of whom held significant positions and not just in Carlisle. When he was eventually brought to trial, it became apparent that he had left a trail of deception from the Sussex coast to the Scottish border.

The prosecution outlined the case against Cave, then called a whole series of witnesses to Cave's various marriages. Cave opted to say nothing in his own defence, refusing to address the court when the judge offered him the chance. The jury had no doubt as to his guilt and Mr Justice Bailey sentenced him to transportation for seven years.

The story doesn't end there, however. Within about a year of landing in Australia, Charles Samuel Cave found himself a fifth wife – Susannah Dockerell (or Dockerall). Perhaps he had at last made his love match, because he did at least wait for Susannah to die before marrying the sixth Mrs Cave, a woman called Elizabeth Hughes, in about 1852. She was to be his last wife as he died before he could marry anyone else.

He also kept up his appetite for a good con during his time in the penal colony in Australia. In March 1827, his then wife Susannah Dockerell, who had herself been transported to the colony, was involved in a scam involving obtaining a 'case of goods', whereby she failed to pay for them. They were valued at £71 11s 1d and Mr Rowe, from whom she had 'bought' the goods, also tried to get the money from the man who was by then her husband, Charles Samuel Cave. The court would hear nothing of the idea that Cave was somehow jointly responsible, but nevertheless found in Mr Rowe's favour and ordered the fifth Mrs Cave to pay up. Then, in 1842, by which time he had crossed the Tasman Sea and was living in New Zealand, Samuel Cave (he had then dropped the Charles) was involved in yet another court case in which he had sold a number of casks of oil. They didn't actually belong to him.

Charles Samuel Cave died on 24 October 1870 in Marlborough, New Zealand. He was about seventy-seven years old at the time – a good age, and had obviously made a strenuous recovery from the terrible heart complaint that had afflicted him when he made the long journey to Carlisle for the sake of his health. Apparently, on his deathbed, he is reported as saying 'he had hardly done anything in his life'.

Of course, the people of Carlisle should have been getting wise to swindlers. They'd already hanged the Keswick Impostor a couple of decades earlier and now the deeds of Charles Samuel Cave would ensure that the population remained vigilant. In October 1824, just two months after the Cave affair had been splashed across both the Carlisle and the National newspapers, the following report appeared in the *Carlisle Journal*:

> *Charles Samuel Cave, Esq. (of Thorney Abbey, Cambridgeshire) had scarcely left our gaol on his way to the hulks, before another* **chevalier d'industrie**, *calling himself Mr Howe, made his appearance in this city and by a specious address and respectable appearance, has succeeded in levying contributions upon some of the inhabitants. He commenced operations in the character of an auctioneer, chiefly for the sale of such horses and carriages as might be entrusted in his care; and having opened an office contiguous to the Bush Inn, advertised in both the Carlisle papers his intention to sell several valuable cattle, an elegant family phaeton and a gig, on the first day of our races. A few days previous to the auction, he disposed of the phaeton (which was the property of a gentleman in this county) to a person in Carlisle for £50, and having effected some minor sales, suddenly decamped with the money...*

You live and learn. Well, most of us do.

Chapter 5

The Death of a Solway Smuggler 1825

For some reason, smuggling has always had an air of romance about it. However, there was nothing truly romantic about the trade at all. Life and limb were often at stake and not simply from the dangers of being caught by the Excise Men, who seemed perfectly happy to fire on suspected contrabandists. Before tax duties were harmonised between Scotland and England, the border regions were populated by smugglers who were involved mainly in the illicit trading of salt and whisky. Many people tried to supplement their income from smuggling, often inventing crafty means of carrying their contraband across the border. Often hearses would be stopped as coffins were a favourite device for the smugglers, who had a running battle with excise men.

Import duties were seen as unfair – certainly the case with the levy on salt (not abolished until 1823), which simply meant that the poor were unable to afford to preserve food for the winter. Furthermore, Excise Men were considered trigger-happy, although there's little evidence to back up this view – they were in danger from the smugglers who could often be ruthless. Nonetheless, local opinion was much more likely to be on the side of the smuggler than the authorities. This sympathy even extended to those men of high enough rank to serve on juries.

The *Carlisle Patriot* of 19 January 1822 carried an article that shows how much such juries could be biased in favour of what was perceived as 'honest' smuggling. Three men of the Preventative Water Guard – Lieutenant Russell, Samuel Kelly and John Hartley – had staked out five suspected smugglers just outside Carlisle. Under the headline 'Melancholy occurrence', the report states that the Preventative Water Guard,

... observed that each man had a package on his back, and Hartley having felt the outside of one of the packages, had no doubt that its contents were Scotch salt, and that all the others contained a similar article. Under this impression, the officers in the king's name, demanded that the packages be delivered up to them, but instead of complying with this demand, the men set upon them with sticks...two of the officers, Russell and Skelly... discharged their pistols at the smugglers and ... William Harding, of Warwick Bridge, was unfortunately shot through the left thigh, the ball coming in contact with the femoral artery, (which) caused his almost immediate death.

An inquest was taken upon the body ... when... contrary to the opinion expressed by the coroner, the jury returned a verdict of murder against John Russell and Samuel Skelly.

If the local jury was on the side of the smugglers, the officers of the Crown were not as convinced. When the case came to the Assizes, the prosecution offered no evidence, which given that the three customs officers had been set about by the gang, seems fair enough by the standards of the justice of the day.

It wasn't just men who were involved either. In early 1827, a woman returning from Scotland had her contraband whisky confiscated by Excise Men. Not wanting to waste her journey entirely, she went back for more, but on her second attempt to get home, wandered off the track onto Solway Moss and died in the snow.

Nor were the boundaries between smuggler and informant neatly drawn. One pair of brothers, Andrew and Francis Forrest, made a living selling contraband Scotch to publicans in North Cumberland, then picked up informants' fees from the Excise Men by shopping the very publicans they had supplied.

In 1825, however, there was a case that would have the neighbourhood divided. On Saturday 15 January, Edward Forster, an Officer of Customs and Excise, was on duty in Kirkandrews-upon-Eden, just to the north-west of Carlisle. He spotted something suspicious on the marshlands of Mossband, next to the River Esk, and when he went to investigate realised that there was smuggling afoot.

He called on George Irving, a local labourer, to come and assist him, explaining that he was an excise officer and both men went off to keep an eye on the supposed smugglers, although they did not see anything during their long, cold night vigil. But the next morning they were hiding behind a bank, when two men and a boy appeared carrying bladders, which Forster reasonably assumed would contain Scotch whisky, as this was a common way of transporting it in those days.

Forster and Irving leapt out from behind their hiding place. Forster seized a man named Charles Gillespie and Irving took hold of a man called Scott. The boy, later identified as William Nixon, who was about fifteen or sixteen, ran off, dropping his load.

The smugglers offered no resistance and Forster and Irving were able to impound their haul of whisky. Gillespie was carrying five-and-a-half gallons of Scotch, which Forster asked Irving to lash to the man's back with a rope, so that there was less likelihood that he could abscond – it was also easier to let the culprit do the heavy work. Irving carried Scott's whisky and Scott in turn carried the whisky that had been dropped by the fleeing Nixon. This meant that Forster wasn't carrying anything, as he was in charge and could thus keep an eye on the others.

Scott and Gillespie had been carrying sticks. Scott's stick was removed, but Gillespie was allowed to keep hold of his – an ash stick about a yard long, that had a knob at one end – presumably to help him carry the bladders containing forty-four pints of Scotch, which would have weighed him down, making it particularly difficult to walk on marshy ground.

Irving and Scott were walking ahead of Forster and Gillespie, heading off towards Esk boathouse, when Scott flung his load of whisky away and ran. Forster called Irving to follow Scott. As Irving belted down the path towards the boathouse, Irving heard a shot and stopped dead. Moments later, there was another shot and then Irving heard Forster calling for him to come back. When he got back to Forster, the excise man was stunned and wiping blood from his head. Forster told Irving that Gillespie had almost killed him and he thought that he had shot him.

Gillespie lay on the ground, supporting himself on his right arm, unable to speak. Irving didn't think that Gillespie was dead at this point. Because blood was gushing from Forster's head, the two men made their way to the boathouse where they were able to get some hand-towels to help staunch the flow. When the bleeding had slowed down, the two men then went back to Gillespie and carried him to the boathouse, but he was dead even before they reached it.

Of course Irving had been out of sight when the shooting happened. The surgeon who examined the body for the coroner's inquest, James Hewitt from Burgh-by-Sands, was unable to tell which of the two wounds had been inflicted first. Gillespie had taken one shot to the upper part of the right thigh and the ball was lodged in the flesh there. His other wound was on the left side of the chest, but he couldn't ascertain exactly where the ball had lodged, believing that it might be wedged in the vertebra somewhere. 'This wound would necessarily cause almost instant death ... I certainly do not think that the man could have stood more than half a minute after receiving the wound in the breast.'

As there must have been doubt as to which wound Gillespie received first, his family also hired the services of a surgeon, a Robert Fraser from Wigton, who had served in Nelson's Navy as a young man. He got to see the body once it had arrived back at Gillespie's house in Wigton and the body had been washed and laid out. He stated in court:

> I have been much used to gunshot wounds in the Navy ... I cannot exactly speak to the person's position who had received such a wound, but I should think it is a leaning back position or the wounded person might have stood on higher ground than he who shot him, otherwise the ball would have taken a downward direction ... the effect of such a wound ...would cause a person to fall; but I can't speak with certainty. The wound, judging from the direction of the ball, might eventually cause death. The next wound was upon the thorax ... on the left side, between the fifth and sixth rib ... I passed a bougie up this wound and found its course through the body towards the spine. Such a wound, I should think, must cause immediate death, for the ball passed through the left lobe of the lungs and perhaps lodged in the spine.

Fraser went on to say that there was bruising to the back of Gillespie's head that he reckoned must have been caused by a blow from a heavy stick from someone standing behind Gillespie and was caused before death.

Forster, as had been predicted, surrendered to the court a few days before he was due to stand trial. The courtroom was packed. According to the *Cumberland Pacquet*, 'most particularly the back part of it where many a trader in whisky anxiously attended to the proceedings'.

Forster's line was that he had shot Gillespie in self-defence with no intention to kill. He pleaded not guilty to the charges and explained that, with blood pouring from his own head wound, he had tussled with his prisoner and genuinely thought that the smuggler was likely to kill him, or had even already dealt him a mortal blow. With all the blood running down his face, he didn't know if his first shot had actually hit Gillespie, especially as he kept on attacking him. After several warnings, he then fired his second shot, the one that hit Gillespie in the chest and killed him.

James Anderson, who attended to both Forster's head wounds and Gillespie's body testified that Forster's injuries were severe and that in places, the stick had cut through the scalp to the skull and that there would have been an awful lot of blood. 'It would require very great violence to produce such a wound by a blunt instrument.' He also had bruises to his hands and arm that Anderson believed would have been caused by raising his arms to defend his head.

Forster also added his own defence:

I lost no time in calling George Irving, and then I went to the boathouse and bound up my head and was very weak from the loss of blood. Afterwards, I went and helped to bring the body to the byre; I sent for a doctor and for the Coroner; nor did I leave the spot till half-past eight at night, when I went to Floristown Bridge and there retired to bed. I solemnly declare that had I not shot the man, he must have taken my life. I owed him no ill will; I entertained no animosity against him, for I never saw him before that day.

One would expect that the court would have been favourably disposed to a man who had both given himself up for trial and had not fled the scene of his alleged crime. It was not to be.

The judge, Mr Justice Holroyd, took one and a half hours to do his summing-up – an extraordinarily long time in those days. Furthermore, in his summing-up, he essentially ruled out the possibility that the verdict be murder and asked the jury to consider whether or not Forster had taken a step too far in shooting Gillespie or that, fearing for his own life, it was a reasonable course of action.

The jury then retired for around twenty minutes to consider their verdict, before declaring Forster guilty of manslaughter, despite the Judge's slanting of his summing-up towards an acquittal. Justice Holroyd then sentenced Forster to one month's imprisonment.

If we are to look again at what happened, the most likely explanation is that Gillespie had taken his stick to Forster, which would explain the free-flowing blood from the excise man's head injury. Knocked to the ground, he would then have been firing upwards, thereby explaining the trajectory of the first pistol ball. If, as Forster suggests, the firing of the shot merely enraged Gillespie into hitting out further, then it is hardly surprising that Forster, after warnings, shot Gillespie for the second time. Gillespie's head injuries could also be caused by blows with the pistol or a stick before Forster, finally enraged, shot Gillespie.

Forster could perhaps console himself that a month in prison was at least better than dangling on the end of a noose.

Chapter 6

Firing on the Mob
1826

When Sir Philip Musgrave of Edenhall, an electoral candidate for Carlisle, went on the hustings to stump up some votes, it was almost unimaginable that his actions would trigger the deaths of three innocent citizens. To say that their election candidate was not particularly liked by some sections of the Carlisle citizenry is an understatement. According to *The Times* of 9 June 1826:

> *Sir Philip is an extremely unpopular candidate, not on account of his personal qualities or demeanour, which I believe are quite unexceptionable, but on account of his politics, and more especially his support of the corn-laws.*

The early nineteenth century was hard for many people. The wars against the French that had started in 1793 had dragged on until the Battle of Waterloo in 1815, gnawing away at the economy and crippling overseas trade. Taxes were (for the times) high, wages depressed and the woollen trade in deep recession. Bad harvests in 1809 and 1811 had made for food shortages. The drift from the country to the towns meant that cities were full of migrant workers. These workers had no choice but to move to larger conurbations as the traditional rural industries could no longer sustain small-scale weaving or spinning in the country as an alternative. Entrepreneurs wanted the economies of scale that the new machinery brought. They weren't going to buy from cottage industries when they could combine all the processes under one roof. One of the traditional means by which rural mini-entrepreneurs had subsidised themselves – keeping a small number of animals on grazing land was no longer possible in many places. Over the centuries, common grazing rights were gradually eroded by various Acts of Parliament and in the preceding few generations, this had been at its height, culminating in the Enclosures Consolidation Act.

And to top it all, there were the Corn Laws. These made it even harder for most of the population, by artificially forcing the price of corn to rise, making the staple of the British diet enormously expensive for the ordinary person. This was an attempt to reduce the dependence and cost of foreign imports and intended to raise productivity at home, but its effects were devastating.

It was certainly a mistake for Sir Philip, a vociferous supporter of the Corn Laws, to go canvassing amongst the few who were then eligible to vote in an area such as Caldewgate. According to one reporter: 'Sir Philip must or ought to have known he was so decidedly unpopular,' as the area of Caldewgate, according to *The Times* of 9 June:

> *... is principally inhabited by persons concerned in cotton manufacture, who are now in a state bordering on starvation, earning from 2s 9d to 4s per week, and whose feelings respecting the corn-laws are most acute. The sight of Sir Philip under such circumstances caused great irritation, and he and his friends were pelted with stones by the rabble. He took refuge in a private house. The mob increased to some hundreds, principally women and boys; but their appearance was sufficiently formidable to prevent Sir Philip attempting to make his way through them.*

As Sir Philip and his entourage took shelter in a building owned by a local merchant, John Cockburn, the mob continued to grow. The Mayor of Carlisle, together with his entourage went down to Caldewgate to see what was going on, but as soon as they got within a hundred yards, they too were bombarded with stones. The mayoral party retreated and the authorities began to pass out muskets to the militia. The *Carlisle Journal* of 10 June takes up the story:

> *About three, a detachment of the 55th Regiment of Foot consisting of unskilled, inexperienced and undisciplined lads, was sent down for the professed purpose of rescuing Sir Philip Musgrave. They went into the heart of Shaddongate and were immediately assailed with a shower of stones; and for the purpose of pelting them, about thirty or forty*

women were seen running about in groups with their aprons full of stones. The soldiers were evidently exasperated and they received orders to fire. They did fire and with a fatal alacrity.

The *Journal* fails to mention one important detail, witnessed by Robert Abraham, a surgeon who would later see one of the victims as she lay dying, and Thomas Carrick, a druggist from Irish-brow. According to Robert Abraham, the militiamen fixed bayonets and charged the mob, which then dispersed, scattering in all directions. It was actually on the backs of the retreating rioters that the militia opened fire. The result of the soldiers' actions was a small-scale massacre. Three people were killed and another boy badly wounded.

The Carlisle journalist who wrote the eyewitness account of the riot that was later re-printed in *The Times*, doesn't give the reader the impression that he was made of the sternest stuff. His article, in which he shadows the activities of the day, is dotted with such phrases as 'I turned and followed at a distance', 'I and two or three acquaintances posted ourselves at a sufficient distance to be out of danger', 'I was told the Riot Act was read, but I was not near enough to ascertain the fact, as I kept aloof near the bridge where I was out of danger,' 'I was not near enough to ascertain the fact.' However, to give him his fair due, he was certainly shocked by what he saw as the rioting died down:

...I was overtaken on my way home by a woman in the greatest agony of grief, who requested me to visit her son-in-law, who was shot. I went with all speed, and found him shot through the chest and bleeding profusely. After doing what was necessary, I left him to see a young woman. She was shot through the temple, her brains escaping through the wound. Assistance was evidently of no use, and I left her to see a boy, about fifteen, who was shot in the heel. I am afraid it will be a bad case; probably the limb will be lost. I then hurried to a young woman, whom I found under the care of a surgeon, who happened, like myself, to be on the spot. She was in the house at the junction of the two streets. A ball had gone completely through the house, entering at one window and going out at another; in its passage it made a terrible fracture of the upper part of her skull. She was trepanned, and the depressed pieces extracted or elevated; but it is very improbable she will survive. I returned to the woman I

mentioned before, and found her dead; the man shot through the body seemed something recovered; there are hopes but feeble ones that the ball has not touched the vital organs. I also heard of another individual being wounded, but did not see him – five in all.

It was a hurried report and our friend, the timid reporter, had not had time to get all the facts together. However, later accounts, including those of the inquests provided the names and greater details of those who had died.

The two young women who had been shot in the head were Isabella Pattinson and Mary Birrell. The surgeon trepanning Isabella was called Mr Thom. According to the *Carlisle Journal*, Mary

… much respected among her neighbours, received a shot while seeking a younger brother in the absence of their mother, with a key in her hand, while she was standing near her own door. The shot came in at the left side of her head, and lodged in the brain. She lived about an hour and twenty minutes afterwards.

As Robert Abraham was later to testify

… I went to see if I could be of any use to Mary Birrell, who I was told was dead, but who I conceived it was possible might have fainted from loss of blood. I found her wounded as above described, and declared to her friends that I could be of no service as the wound was mortal, and she at the time in a dying state, though she continued to breathe for an hour afterwards.

Mary was twenty-two years old and, as with all the others, had nothing at all to do with the riot that was in progress. Isabella was even younger. The *Carlisle Journal* told her story in these terms:

One of the soldiers was observed to load and reload his piece and at the last fire, he sent a ball through the window shutter and window of a parlour across the front room, through the back part of the head of a poor innocent girl who was in the school at the time. The girl, whose name was Isabella Pattinson, instantly fell, never to rise again.

At the coroner's inquest, Dinah Clarke, the school-mistress who owned the little dame school in Shaddongate, gave the following evidence:

The deceased, Isabella Pattinson, was at my door on Tuesday last. I brought her and a number of little ones into the school-room for safety, when I saw the soldiers coming on the Bridge [Caldew Bridge]. I then closed the window of the school-room. The deceased was not one of my scholars, but my sister brought her in amongst the rest. I bolted the door, and afterwards went into the school-room and expressed to the children how thankful I was that we were all safe ... Isabella Pattinson was standing on the floor at some distance from the window with two other little girls – they had hold of each others' hands – the deceased was in the middle. I went to see that the door was properly fastened. When I returned, the other children had all retired into a back room and I found the deceased lying on the floor. She told me she had been shot. I lifted her up into my arms and endeavoured to take her to the passage door to get a little air; but finding it impossible to take her any further on account of weakness.

Mrs Clarke went for a towel and sent for both Isabella's brother Richard and the doctor – Mr Thom. Isabella had been shot through the window and there was nothing that Mr Thom could do except dress the wound. By eight o'clock, Isabella was dead. She was fourteen years old.

Two separate inquests were carried out on the three victims. That of Isabella Pattinson and Mary Birrell took place at the *Joiner's Arms* on Caldewgate just a few days later. Robert Noble took a little longer to die. Both inquests were guardedly critical of the authorities. This was the verdict of the first:

That the deaths of the deceased, Isabella Pattinson and Mary Birrell, were occasioned by balls discharged from muskets by some soldier or soldiers belonging to the 55th Regiment of Foot. That, in consequence of the Riot Act having been read, and the mob not dispersing, the soldiers were, in the first instance, justified in firing their muskets; but the jurors cannot refrain from expressing their opinion, that they continued to fire in a very indiscreet and inconsiderate manner, and particularly at private houses, when the necessity for so doing seems to them to have ceased. That their deaths were in other respects accidental.

In a sad twist, the funeral processions of Isabella Pattinson and Mary, which had gathered a huge crowd of mourners, pall-bearers all dressed in white, passed by the windows of the *Joiner's Arms* at the very time that the inquest was taking place.

If the inquests into Isabella and Mary's deaths were critical, then would that into the death of Robert Noble apportion any blame? Like Isabella and Mary, Nobel had nothing to do with the riot, a fact corroborated by several witnesses. It was also confirmed by the surgeon who attended Nobel, who testified that the dying man had told him that he had nothing to do with the riots – evidence that was ruled inadmissible by the coroner as the dying man's statement had not been witnessed by a magistrate.

One witness, William Wilson, a weaver who lived in Queen Street, gave evidence at both inquests. He went so far as to testify that he had seen one of the militiamen, a Private Irving, raise his gun and deliberately shoot Noble, although his evidence differed slightly between the two inquests and at the second he amended his statement slightly to say that although he had not seen the shot fired, he could tell from Irving's position and the way he held his musket, that it was he who had fired the shot.

Despite any evidence to the contrary, the verdict on Noble was 'accidental death occasioned by a musket-shot fired by a soldier unknown after the reading of the Riot Act'.

Of course, deaths like these are the result of a series of events and contributing factors. However, the Carlisle Riots and their aftermath illustrate the inevitable result of politicians who won't listen to opinion, disdain for those members of society least able to look after themselves and an ill-trained force expected to police an extraordinarily volatile situation. This was Carlisle's very own Peterloo Massacre.

The Times report of 26 June 1826 was scathing:

It has appeared from the enquiry already made that all the persons concerned had no concern whatever with the riot … We will take it for granted (although it is no means certain) that in each of these cases the killing was accidental, but that circumstances in our minds forms the great objection to military interference. It is because the application of military force is from its very nature at once indiscriminate and deadly that the law discountenances it, and common sense and justice abhor it. It is true that force must be repelled by force; but there is no maxim in law more clear than this – that no man is justified in resorting to excessive force ... It is not (as it is so often erroneously supposed) the reading of the Riot Act which invests them [magistrates] with such extraordinary powers: the Riot Act merely puts the rioters in a new position with respect to the penalties of law. By converting the trespassers who disobey it into felons; but though the rioter becomes a felon, he is a felon to be tried by a jury and condemned by a jury, before he can be punished: he is not a mad dog, to be shot at by the first gun that can be levelled against him.

Without doubt, the militiamen of Carlisle were very quick indeed to level their guns. As for the election itself – it was won by Sir James Graham, who polled 118 votes. It seems that the anti-Musgrave vote was split in two by the late arrival of a third candidate, William James. Nonetheless, Sir Philip was beaten into second place, garnering only 91 votes.

The incident left an unpleasant taste in the mouths of many. It also showed the lack of understanding that many politicians had of the conditions in which a good proportion of the people of the country lived. Yet, it was more than twenty years before the Corn Laws were eventually repealed and common grazing rights continued to be eroded. Meanwhile, Isabella Pattinson, Mary Birrell and Robert Noble were the victims of some particularly rough justice.

Chapter 7

Sarah Fox and the Poisoned Coffee 1826

Usually if there is poison involved in a husband-wife murder case, it is the wife who has administered it. In the case of Sarah Fox, it was her husband who gave her the fatal dose. The wonderfully-named Mary Pharaoh, had been invited to a christening party at a near-neighbour's house on 16 September 1826 and had arrived there at about 5 o'clock. About two and a half hours later, Robert Fox, her son-in-law, came to the house and told her that she needed to come home because her two daughters, Sarah and Margaret, were very ill. Fox was worried that Sarah wouldn't live till the morning, as she was particularly poorly.

Mary Pharaoh, whom we should imagine was having a good time and had had enough drink to be feeling both mellow and unwilling to be dragged away from the party, followed Robert home, pooh-poohing his suggestions of how ill the two young women were. After all, she reasoned, with Sarah so far pregnant it was more than likely that she was having the first signs of labour and she knew that Margaret had a 'trifling cold'.

John and Mary Pharaoh shared their house with their children, including Sarah and their son-in-law, Robert. John was not particularly well-paid, earning his living as a waller and general labourer. When she got home, Mary Pharaoh could see her daughters were genuinely ill. Sarah explained that Robert had made her coffee by heating up what had been left from the morning's brew. It had tasted bad, so he had put more sugar in it, complaining to her that it was just 'one of her fancies' – pregnant women often disliking the taste of coffee. But when Margaret also tried some she was ill, so they threw the lot in the pigswill and when the pig ate it, the poor porker was also poorly.

In her statement to the inquest into Sarah's death, which was held at Bankhouse in Gosforth, Mary Pharaoh reported what she did as follows:

I considered hyssop tea would be of service in allaying sickness, and made some and took it to my youngest daughter, who said that it had the same bad taste as the coffee. I thought the bad taste complained of arose from the water having stood in the kettle the whole of the day. I therefore washed the kettle well out, and made some more cups of tea, of which they both drank, and thought it good. I then asked the deceased if she would eat any thing and she replied in the affirmative. I made her a posset of milk, bread, and beer, of which she ate, and said it was very good, and what was left she would take after a bit. Robert, her husband, desired me to go to bed, and he would take care of her till the morning.

Sarah was ill all during the evening and the following Sunday. In the early hours of Monday morning, she gave birth to a still-born child, described by Mary Pharaoh as being 'all black' (arsenic can poison a child in the womb). Sarah continued to be ill, complaining of a burning throat. She drank pint after pint of water as well as beer, which would probably have been pretty watery stuff and regarded as a normal everyday beverage, much the same as we might nowadays drink a glass of squash.

All the time, she insisted that her husband, Robert, had put something into her coffee to make her feel bad. She even went so far as to accuse him of having bought something in Whitehaven that he'd then put in her cup. The poor woman lasted another twenty-four hours before dying on the Tuesday, three days after she'd been poisoned.

At the inquest, Fox denied ever having been near a 'druggist's', but a certain Mr Saul was to give evidence otherwise. He said:

*I am a druggist in Whitehaven, and perfectly remember FOX calling at my shop, on Thursday, the 14th of September. He wanted some arsenic, he said, for killing rats. I refused to let him have it, but in consequence of a person who was in the shop at the time saying he knew him, I sold him what he asked for, and wrapped it up in three different papers, and wrote the word **poison** upon them, to prevent any accident.*

On top of that, the inquest also heard from several medical men who had been present at the post-mortem examination:

Mr Wright of Gosforth, opened the body, in the presence of Messrs. THOMPSON and DAWSON, of Whitehaven, and Mr LAWSON, of Egremont, who were all of opinion that the deceased came to her death by poison.

The inquest, inevitably, decided that Sarah Fox had been murdered and also that Robert Fox should be tried for administering arsenic.

By the standards of the day, Fox had a long time to wait before he was tried at Carlisle Assizes. It wasn't until Friday 9 March 1827, almost six months after Sarah's death, that Fox appeared in front of Baron Hullock. The trial served to reinforce what had already been said at the inquest, with several further witnesses – Mary Briggs and Ann Cormick, two Gosforth women, confirming that they had all seen Sarah as the poison had taken hold along with her dead baby, again described as being somewhat blackened.

David Saul, the druggist repeated his earlier evidence from the inquest, adding that he had a rule that he wouldn't sell poison to anyone he didn't know. As he didn't know Fox, he had been reluctant to sell him arsenic. However, a man called John James happened to be in the shop at the same time and he was known to both David Saul and Robert Fox, so he vouched for Fox to the druggist, joking to Fox, 'What, are you going to poison your wife already?'

Then came a key witness, a Henry Bertuff. He had overheard a conversation between Fox and another of Sarah's sisters, Hannah. Hannah had asked how Sarah was and Fox had replied that she was poorly, but he had bought her stuff in Whitehaven the previous Thursday. It hadn't however done any good, but only given her a 'good heckling'.

This could not be a case of accidental poisoning. Fox offered no defence and the jury didn't even leave the courtroom, only 'turning round for a moment' before reaching their guilty verdict.

When Baron Hullock pronounced the death sentence, Fox asked if he could address the court. He said, 'Well, gentlemen, I am willing to give up my life for the life that I have taken. The taking of my wife's life was nothing to taking that of my child. I ask no favour. The Lord brought me into the world, and I hope he will take me out of it.'

Fox was sentenced to hang in a double-bill with Phillip Tinnaney, whose name is also reported as Tinnary and Finnacey. Tinnaney, a middle-aged market-trader, was known to visit Mary Brown, who was a twenty-six-year-old woman, in her lodgings. Unfortunately, her affections wandered towards someone nearer her own age (apparently they often did) and in a drink-fuelled row, he beat her severely around the head with the proverbial blunt instrument. It took the poor woman a good day to die – a little speedier than Sarah Fox – and although Tinnaney fled from the scene, he took people back to help her, showing remorse for what he had done.

Tinnaney had also nearly pulled off a neat trick in court, when he appeared on the same day as Fox. Asked how he pleaded, he refused to do so on religious grounds: if he said he was not guilty, he would be lying and if he said he was guilty, then he was essentially committing suicide, which was an immoral act. Obviously, it didn't help his cause a great deal, as can be seen from the report in *The Times*, in which he is referred to as Finnacey. With all the solemnity one would expect of a serious newspaper whose readers nonetheless wanted some titillation the double execution was described in *The Times* of 17 March 1827:

The prisoners walked with a firm pace, and raised their eyes until they beheld the engine of death, which they surveyed with a seemingly unshaken fortitude; and then, with downcast countenances, moved on till they arrived at the door of the stairs by which they were to ascend to the roof of the prison. Here the Governor of the gaol took the charge of Fox, and the turnkey held Finnacey, as if to assist him up the stairs of the prison, and up the ladder of the machine, if he should require assistance. They arrived in this order upon the drop. The ropes had been adjusted about their necks before they left their cells; and their arms were pinioned above the elbow. Fox's rope was now immediately attached to the chain; but Finnacey knelt down with his minister on stools that had been provided, for the purpose of concluding his devotions with his latest breath, and prayed aloud for nearly ten minutes. During this time, Fox held some conversation with the Ordinary, in a whisper or undertone, that was inaudible even to those immediately below the drop, and he trembled very much. Finnacey's devotions being concluded, he rose up, and was placed by the side of his fellow sufferer; and his rope being attached to the chain [which in turn would have been attached to the gibbet], at about 12 minutes past 12 the executioner did his duty. A slight tremulous motion, probably resulting from that which had been previously observed in Fox, agitated his body for several minutes during his suspension; but nothing like a struggle, nor even the ordinary contortions which might have been expected by bodies dying by suffocation, could at any time be perceived, in either of the present cases. It is, therefore, rather conjectured, that death was immediately caused in both by vertebral fracture. The bodies are to be dissected this afternoon. Fox appeared a man who had acquired, by a gross life, an habitual insensibility to the common sympathies of our nature. He had contracted an illicit intercourse with a young woman whom, in the seventh month of her pregnancy, he was induced to marry, after the parish-officers had interfered in the matter; and whom, with a cold blooded purpose, he deliberately poisoned in the ninth month.

The execution on that March day was witnessed by thousands of people – the only thing better than a hanging was a double hanging. The fact that it took Fox a good few minutes to die as he dangled on the end of too short a rope made it all the more fun for the crowd.

Chapter 8

The Mysterious Death of Barnaby Burns 1834

On 10 October 1834, Barnaby Burns went to the Cockermouth Fair. It was the last time he would be seen alive. The next day, he was missing from the Workington Colliery where he worked carting coal. A week later, his bruised and battered body, probably dumped further upstream and carried over the weir by the swollen waters of the River Derwent, came to rest against the pillars of the bridge in Cockermouth. He was still wearing fustian trousers, a blue coat and waistcoat and two shirts – one chequered, one white, torn roughly at the neck.

Somewhere along the line, despite some shaky evidence, the authorities concluded that he had been murdered. In *The Times*

The River Derwent at Cockermouth, where the body of Barnaby Burns was found.

report of the criminal trial held the year following his death, a local man called John Fawcett, from Great Broughton, described finding the body:

> *On the 17th of October last, I saw the body of a man from the bridge, on the Cockermouth side, against the pillars of the bridge. There were near five feet of water. I gave information, got assistance, and the body was taken out in my presence. I examined it generally. There was a large cut on the left temple, the left breast was all bruised, and there was a small cut on the other side of the head, and a cut on the forehead. I can't tell if it was sufficient to kill a man. It was two inches one way, and one the other. The skull bone was bare.*

The men carried the body along to a nearby barn and called for William Bracken, a shoemaker in the town, to come and identify the deceased. He confirmed it was Barnaby Burns. At the coroner's inquest, held on 19 October, Joseph Dickenson, a Workington surgeon, was asked to examine the body, which was at Burns's father's house. For some reason, the inquest jury would not allow him to cut open the body, but from his examination of Burns's external injuries, he stated:

> *I don't consider that these wounds would cause death instantly. If I had opened the head, I do not think I could have formed a better opinion of the cause of death, the body was so decomposed.... The skin was in a flabby state, very loose. I did not try if it was easily torn. The skin of the long wound flapped over, and the edges were rugged. The wound might have been formed after death by the body being floated against a stake of the wear or against any edged substance. The wound, though not sufficient to cause instant death, might cause concussion of the brain so as to produce death afterwards, but I can't say whether that wound would or would not produce death.*

Nevertheless, a young man was dead. The jury at the trial would hear evidence from which they could piece together a hazy picture of Barnaby Burns's last day.

October the 10th was a Thursday and the Cockermouth fair provided everyone with a local holiday. Barnaby Burns, who was around twenty-four or twenty-five at the time of his death, decided that the best possible use he could make of it was to knock back as

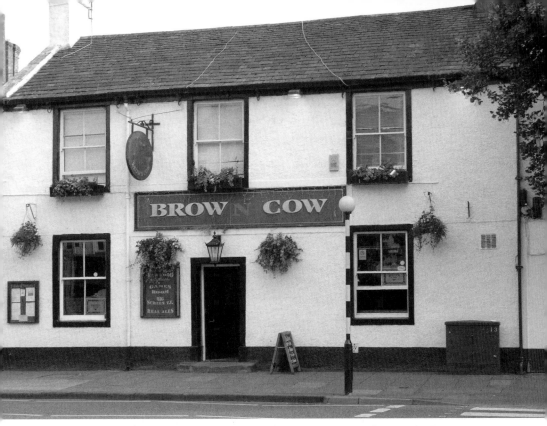

The Brown Cow *in Cockermouth – one of the many pubs in which Barnaby Burns was seen drinking on the night of his disappearance.*

much as he could and had begun his drinking spree early.

At the trial, Margaret Thompson, who obviously knew Barnaby Burns reasonably well, told the jury that:

I met Barnaby Burns in Cowen's tent on the hill where the fair was. It was afternoon. He gave me a glass of gin there, and we came down together. We parted at the Brown Cow door in the evening. I saw him again a little after 12. I was going down to the bridge to meet a gentleman… He was alone, I went up to him. He said he'd been in a scrape since he had seen me. He said Stanwix, the constable, had used him ill. He took off his hat and asked me to feel his head. There was a 'blunge' in his head. It was behind the ear. Some person came up and I left him there.

The Lowther Inn, from which Barnaby Burns was later ejected, was just one of the several places that he had supped in that day and night.

Margaret Thompson's testimony went on to place him in the

early hours of the morning at a little after 2 o'clock by the Derwent Bridge. He then got himself into an argument with a group of men, who started to pull and push him about. During the encounter, Burns had apparently tried to placate his attackers, but they would have none of it. They knocked him to the ground, kicked him where he fell and one of them set about him with the thick end of a cart-whip. When they had finished all that, they picked him up and threw him over the fence into the Derwent.

That there had been some kind of commotion in the area was corroborated by a local tailor, Richard Black, and evidence of the ferocity of the attack was supported by a young worker at Pitt's Mill, Esther Taylor. The day after the fight, she was on her way to work with her sister Jane and spotted blood all over the area where Margaret Thompson had reported the incident took place. Esther, using the word her father had explained to her, called the blood 'coggilated' (we must assume she meant 'coagulated'). A rail, apparently removed from the fence next to the river, was lying in the mill yard. Bloody hand-prints covered it.

It took a year – an extraordinarily long time by the standards of the day – for anyone to be brought to court for the alleged homicide. In the end, five men, including three from the same family, were charged with the murder. Thomas, William and Walter Nicholson, Joseph Green and George Burgess were all charged with the wilful murder of Barnaby Burns. They worked alongside Barnaby Burns at the Workington pit as carters. There were plenty of witnesses to put them in Cockermouth on the night of the Michaelmas Fair – a fact that none of them denied – and many more who had seen them move towards the area along the Workington Road out of Cockermouth near where the fracas took place.

The trial did not finish until ten o'clock at night. The court had been packed out all day, such was the interest it had aroused. With five men on trial, there were also plenty of family and friends there to lend support.

Knowing Barnaby Burns' drunken state and having heard the evidence, the jury, after retiring for a short deliberation, brought in a verdict of not guilty. Given that Joseph Dickenson, the

Workington surgeon, had explained to the coroner's inquest that he couldn't determine fully the cause of death, then it's surprising that the case even got to court. Whilst the authorities could determine that there had been some kind of fracas, there was no evidence whatsoever that a murder had occurred.

One other difficulty must have been that the star witness for the prosecution – Margaret Thompson – did not have an entirely unblemished reputation. Her behaviour, by the standards of the day, was not beyond criticism and in her testimony, she admitted that she no longer lived with her husband, had spent twelve months in Carlisle Gaol and 'would rather not say if I am of any trade or profession'. She also referred to several 'gentlemen' whom she didn't know by name and was 'on the Papcastle Road between 12 and 2 o'clock" (in the morning). According to her testimony, she had been in the company of Barnaby Burns, a certain Edward Parkins ('I spent part of the night in his company') and at least one other man. I don't think it would be unfair of us to conclude that Margaret was a prostitute and that Cockermouth Fair would have been a potentially big pay-day for her. Whilst some of the jury might have been amongst those who would appreciate her services, they were unlikely to rely on her evidence.

Her testimony was further undermined by the fact that she had earlier sworn twice on oath that she had no idea what had happened to the body. In court, her testimony had changed for no obvious reason. Even though her new version was partially supported by that of Richard Black, who had earlier been drinking himself in the *Sun Inn*, it remained unconvincing.

An alibi was provided for George Burgess by William Allison, and the unimaginatively-named John Johnson provided one for Joseph Green. These alibis were also confirmed by other witnesses, including a certain William Wordsworth – not the poet, but one of his relatives – possibly a cousin. This meant that two of the alleged five could not have been at the spot alongside the River Derwent where the fight took place.

On the other hand, the general standard of the witness testimony for the prosecution was, to be generous, confused. Anyone who believes that British binge-drinking is a modern phenomenon would be much mistaken. Much of the evidence presented to the court was from people who had spent the whole of that day drinking themselves into various states of stupefaction and could not be relied upon as witnesses.

How Barnaby Burns died remains something of a mystery. The most likely explanation is that, having got into a fight, and befuddled by drink and possibly concussed, he was either thrown or simply stumbled into the River Derwent. If the blows he received were part of the cause of his death, might the earlier blow he received off Stanwix, the Constable, have been to blame? After all, he complained about the state of his head to Margaret Thompson several hours before he got into the fight. Of course, because Mr Dickenson was unable to carry out a full post-mortem examination by opening up the body, he would not be able to tell if death was from drowning (the most likely cause of death). It still, of course, wouldn't answer the hoary old question 'did he fall or was he pushed?' According to Margaret Thompson, he was pushed. She had nothing to gain from giving this evidence, and everything to lose by appearing in court and laying what little reputation she had on the line.

As it is, Barnaby Burns's death remains a mystery.

Chapter 9

The Rampant Curate of Rampside
1835

The parishioners of Rampside on the Furness Peninsula must have been pleased when their advertisement in the *Cumberland Pacquet* brought them a young, newly-married curate and his wife.

The advertisement had read 'Curate Wanted. Wanted a Curate for the Chapelry of Rampside in the County of Lancaster; a Title will be given to a Respectable Young man if required'. A 'title' was essentially a promise that the incumbent would be eligible for ordination by the Bishop, although the stipend for this kind of position was not large. You didn't have to have much in the way of qualifications to be a curate in the early nineteenth century. It was enough to be male, literate and of the Christian religion (note that you only had to be 'of' the religion, you didn't actually have to believe in any of it). Often the youngest sons of wealthy families, subsidised by allowances from the parental purse or small inheritances, would take these jobs, but Rampside wasn't the most attractive parish for the scions of England's finest. However, the locals were perfectly happy that they had their new man and that he was right for the job.

Their new curate was John Stainton. He had been born in Egremont, that Cumbrian rarity – a town with a name derived from the French – in 1785. His father, a stonemason, lived at Orepit House in Bigrigg and young John probably attended St Bees School, although there is no firm record of his having done so. Nonetheless his level of literacy was good for the age in which he lived and he seemed an appropriate match for Eleanor Haile, a few years his senior. She too was a stonemason's daughter.

In 1808, Stainton and his wife arrived in Rampside, but his poor

St Michael's church, Rampside where our randy, rampant curate was the priest – when not suspended or in gaol.

Eleanor gave birth to a stillborn child not long afterwards and never recovered, dying herself only a few weeks later without really getting out of the bed in which she had given birth. John Haile, her father, then demanded repayment of the dowry that had accompanied Eleanor. This was beyond Stainton's pocket. There was no way in which a local curate could afford to pay the money and Stainton's own father was initially unable to help.

Unable to pay, Stainton was whisked away to the debtors' wing at Carlisle Gaol, thereby missing the original date for his ordination. Eventually, Stainton's father managed to scrape together the wherewithal to pay what his son owed Haile, and Stainton returned to Rampside. He was ordained in September 1811, having re-married the previous March. His new bride was Ann Huddleston, a servant of Richard Pemberton, who owned the large estate at Page Bank. Richard Pemberton seems to have been very good to his young curate, supporting him through these difficult times. His new wife couldn't have been bad to him either, producing twelve children over the next few years, of whom four were to die in infancy.

However, when Richard Pemberton died and the estate moved on to his son Robert, the estate failed to pay its tithe to the church – meaning that Stainton would again have been short of money. There was a court case over this dispute, which Stainton won. A year or so later, when Robert died Page Bank was in the hands of his brother, another Richard Pemberton, who also seems to have looked kindly on a man who was about to become very wayward indeed.

During Stainton's second marriage, his drinking began to infuriate the locals. They petitioned the Bishop of Chester, under whose diocese Rampside fell, to do something about their vicar's behaviour. Stainton was duly summoned to Chester to explain his actions, but the Bishop was not fully convinced and later travelled to visit him at Rampside to see for himself what his turbulent priest was up to. Up to something he must have been, because he was promptly suspended from duty for two years.

Reinstated, Stainton then got into a fight on the beach over some seaweed with a local man, Thomas Storey. Again, there was a court case over the incident, brought by Stainton against Storey. But it was dismissed for lack of evidence, as everyone who was a witness was partial to one side or the other. However, he was becoming even more wayward and protests at his behaviour were now commonplace. His parishioners were driven to complain yet again to episcopal authority. They got up a petition about their curate and in July 1830, the case against John Stainton was heard at the Consistory Court at Richmond, a consistory court being one at which the trial of any clergy who have been alleged to have acted immorally is heard.

Facing John Stainton were allegations of 'profanity, drunkenness, incontinence, immorality, lewd and indecent conduct and conversation, neglect and misbehaviour in his clerical duties'. As a blow to the Church of England's status in an area where nonconformism was already popular, many of his parishioners were driven across to worship with the Methodists and 'even the servants were reluctant to attend' Stainton's services.

The charges paint a picture of a Stainton that any pirate on shore leave would have been proud to emulate. In those days, Ulverston,

Daltongate, Ulverston – the Reverend John Stainton was known to frequent Martha Armstrong's brothel in this road.

not Barrow-in-Furness, was the major town on the Furness Peninsula. It was here that Stainton came in order to indulge his various vices. The Reverend Stainton enjoyed his drink. He was often seen in the *Braddylls Arms*, the *Sun Inn* and other local hostelries. When in his cups, he would often become lewd and suggestive and was witnessed to shove his hand up one poor woman's skirt. That was if he could remain conscious. On at least one occasion, the constables found him staggering round Ulverston, before collapsing in a heap. His personal hygiene seems to have deserted him too, as the landlord of the *Braddylls Arms*, Henry Braithwaite, accused him of 'using the dining-room as a privy'.

The Braddylls Arms, *Ulverston. John Stainton frequently drank here, until barred for using the dining-room as a toilet.*

He was known to have visited prostitutes throughout the town. He was a frequent visitor to Anne Pattie in Canal Street, Jane Taylor's house in Soutergate, which was known to be used as a house of ill-repute, and Martha Armstrong's brothel in Daltongate. He was also seen in the company of Mary Tyson, who was 'a woman of the town'.

In all, thirty-one people gave testimony as to Stainton's wayward behaviour. Given the number of depositions made against him, it was always unlikely that Stainton would retain his job and he was duly suspended again – this time for three years. He took his large family to live on the Page Bank Estate, where he was loaned a house by Richard Pemberton.

Then, Pemberton died. The estate should have passed on to the nearest male relative. In this case, the beneficiary was a John Fazakerley, and it was obvious to Stainton that he would be turfed out by the new owner. Stainton had no money and nowhere else to go, so he moved onto the next stage of his career – forgery. With Pemberton's 'will' in his hands, he refused to allow Fazakerley to enter Page Bank, which was worth around £3,000 – the equivalent to anywhere between £3 and £7 million at today's prices. Page Bank was worth keeping in the family and Stainton intended to keep it in his.

But Stainton was caught out by changing his story. He had Pemberton's will, leaving all the estate to him, and also insisted that Pemberton had made him the executor as well. However, it would appear that traditionally, as well as there being a will, there would also have been a further document called a 'deed of surrender of the uses of the will'. When John Fazakerley asked Stainton if there was a deed of surrender in the August of the previous year, Stainton said there wasn't. A fortnight later, however, he was able to produce such a document miraculously dated the same day as the will.

Eventually, the case came to Lancaster Assizes on 23 March 1835. John Crank, an Ulverston solicitor, swore that the signature was not Pembertons's as did several others. It was also shown that the deed was stamped about two years after it was purported to have been. *The Times* correspondent, perhaps heaving a sigh for how soft the law had become of late, reported that:

The learned JUDGE observed that the prisoner would, a few years ago, have been liable to death for this offence, and there was strong reason to believe that the will was also forged, and he ought to think himself fortunate that he had not been indicted for that which would subject him to the punishment of death. Under these circumstances, he thought it proper that he should be transported for life.

Transportation certainly wasn't a soft option. Writing a decade after Stainton was deported, a Mr R Williams, who was aboard one of the convict ships, wrote to his family, describing his ship thus:

A ship for male convicts is more strongly fitted and guarded than one for females ... It is fitted with 2 tiers of sleeping berth all round so as to lay athwart-ships and only 14 inches wide for each by 6 feet long, therefore 6 feet from each side of this ship will have a space of about 10 feet wide, where hammocks will be hung in case there is not sufficient berths. So being thus managed, a great number are stowed in a very small place. In the after end of the prison there are holes made for the soldiers to fire on them if they are unruly, there is also a necessary house on each side forward on deck with holes in for the same purpose from which there is only a passage for one man at a time. Round the hatchways between decks are secured with strong Elm posts fitted with broad headed nails so that they cannot cut or anyway injury them. There is also a place about 12 feet by 10 feet fitted for an hospital in case of sickness. From the prison to the stern on the same deck are all the sailors and soldiers with a partition between.

Today the first draught 100 came down from Dublin in a steamboat being guided by policemen, each convict being well shackled by the legs but with their hands free. Just before they came to us, our soldiers mounted the poop and loaded their guns all ready. They were then passed one by one on board, had their clothes searched for knives, razors, matches, tobacco and passed the doctor who took their names and sent them down to the prison and they had not been there long before one got his ……. and flute and began playing, and the others began dancing a hornpipe. All this kept up until it was dark. They are all really very young, some of them quite lads, a few elderly men who I understand are nearly all old soldiers,

The Sun Inn, *Ulverston, where John Stainton liked to go carousing.*

1 old man and 2 of his sons with him ... I will just describe their dress, they have flannel singlets, striped cotton shirts, drab cloth jacket, breeches and waistcoat, woollen stockings, good shoes, cotton kerchiefs and woollen caps. They are not allowed to get wet. There are some left to cook for the others. Their allowance is certainly small, being at the rate of 4 men's allowance for 6 according to a Man of War, but no spirits and no wine, but in case of sickness. There is no difference in the treatment or clothing for heavy crimes or light crimes, the only difference being in the length of the sentence.

... Today at 2 pm our 2nd draught of prisoners came on board, being 100 in number, the same precautions were taken as before or rather more strict in consequence of some of the others having eluded the search and got a razor down into the prison, together with some Lucifer matches, for which the first lot were searched a second time.

This lot, like the other, is for the most part very young, some of them being quite little lads – but such lads you could fancy you could see the gallows in their visages. I was thinking this afternoon that a good phisiognomist would have a good opportunity of exercising his talents in reading the characters of so many bare-faced, impudent wretches. But it may be that some, even among these, are more unfortunate than dishonest, one there is a soldier who has got 14 years merely for striking a sergeant ... One man came today with his little boy, not more than 5 years of age. The boy is of course under no sentence. Another with a little boy in petticoats, perhaps about 2½ or 3 years of age, this man I'm told has 2 little girls which are to come out shortly in another ship which is to take female convicts, perhaps their mother amongst them.

This voyage out will of course be a very unpleasant one being so crowded, no less than 304 persons in all in a ship of only 500 tons with provisions and water for six months and not allowed to call anywhere if it can be avoided. The worst of my fears are of being becalmed on the Line with only 3 quarts of water a man under a hot sun, would be hard lines I tell you.

Stainton was sent to the penal colony at Port Macquarie, where he was given a job in the hospital and regarded as 'special', because he was obviously an educated man rather than from the 'lower orders'. He eventually died in around 1848-50, by which time he had received a pardon, but hadn't been to collect it. His widow died in Ulverston in 1856.

Chapter 10

The Razor-grinder's Wife
1844

n a hard December night in 1844, Thomas Donahoo staggered from his home in Hart Street, Ulverston to his sister-in-law's house. 'I'm afraid my wife is dead,' he told her.

It was a bit of an understatement. No-one seeing the state of the body of Ellen Donahoo could come to any other conclusion. According to *The Times*, at the inquest held a week after the incident, on 28 December, Mr Barton, a local surgeon, testified that ...

>*...there were three wounds on the deceased's head, any one of which could have proved fatal, but that the immediate cause of death was a severe wound on the back part of the head, which might have been done by some obtuse instrument. He found about a spoonful of extravasated blood pressing on the brain. He also stated that the whole body, especially the legs, thighs and arms, was severely bruised; and on being shown a piece of square iron, round at the ends like a pivot, he said that the marks and bruises corresponded with the iron, he having measured them with it ...He also distinctly stated that the deceased could not possibly have received such wounds by falling down stairs, as stated by the prisoner...*

The iron bar that the surgeon was given to examine was probably the spindle for a grinding-wheel, the square cross-section acting as a kind of axle for the polishing wheel. Mr Barton seemed satisfied that this was the murder weapon as ' ... he had particularly examined the iron, and was confident there was a spot of blood on the end; and that it had the appearance of being recently washed as the bright part of the iron was somewhat oxidized.'

Hart Street, Ulverston, where Thomas Donahoo lived with the wife he would kill.

It didn't look good for Donahoo. He had been arrested straight away and the inquest would soon hear that there was only one likely outcome from their enquiry into the sorry business.

The most damning evidence came from Donahoo's twelve-year-old son, who asked to be allowed to make a statement. He told the inquest that his father had abused his mother, kicking her and hitting her both up and down the stairs, dragging her by the hair and 'in various other ways abusing her'. *The Times* correspondent reporting the inquest reckoned that Donahoo's son's evidence '...will probably when given elsewhere consign the parent to an ignominious death'.

Donahoo was inevitably sent for trial at Lancaster – in those days Ulverston was part of Lancashire. He was brought before Justice Coleman at the Lancaster Spring Assizes of 1845. There was little in the way of mitigation for Donahoo, whose poor children were by now living in the workhouse in Ulverston.

From the evidence given at the inquest and at the later trial, it seems that the Donahoos were not the happiest couple in the little market town.

Donahoo, whose name variously appears as Donoghue, Donough and Donoghoo, was an itinerant razor-grinder and tinker, who had settled temporarily in Ulverston. He lived with his wife, Ellen, and his two children, a boy and a girl aged tweve and three; four other children had died in infancy. According to the *Lancaster Gazette* of 4 January 1845 'it seems the prisoner and his wife lived on the most wretched terms and their brawls were of frequent reoccurrence'. Too poor even to afford proper mattresses, the Donahoos slept on piles of straw on the floor. Almost every word they uttered could be heard through the feeble walls of the house, especially as Donahoo tended to shout as he was deaf.

Ulverston was, before the rise of Barrow-in-Furness, the major town of the Furness Peninsula, and its narrow streets were a maze of rough dwellings, brothels and ale houses. It was here that the Donahoos spent what little spare money they had on drink. Ellen Donahoo especially liked to dance in the public houses and often returned home drunk.

On the night of the killing, a local policeman, Constable Sandwell, had been on duty in the town. One suspects from his various statements to the inquest and at the trial that he knew the Donahoos and that this was not the first time he had had to intervene in their domestic affairs.

He had seen an unbruised Ellen Donahoo staggering drunk around the town between midnight and one in the morning on her way back to her house. When he later encountered Donahoo, he told the razor-grinder that his wife had gone home. Donahoo obviously hadn't finished drinking for the night and wanted more money, so told Sandwell that we would 'go home and give her a good licking'. Obviously worried for Ellen Donahoo's safety, Constable Sandwell called round at the house a short while later, where he found Donahoo ranting about his wife's behaviour (she had used his drinking money to get drunk herself) and claiming that he had knocked her off a stool and then searched her for money, but found none. Donahoo then '... took a can, apparently having water in it, and a cloth, and began washing about the foot of the stairs.' Donahoo also took out what appeared to be a stone and rubbed the floor with that before going back upstairs to the part of the house in which they lived. Sandwell heard moaning from the room above, but didn't investigate any further.

However, if Constable Sandwell thought that this was just one of the Donahoo's regular brawls, he was mistaken. All was not well. From the other side of the thin lath and plaster wall that separated the Donahoos from their neighbour, James Walker, a shoemaker:

> ... *could hear any ordinary conversation going on. When he awoke he found that Donahoo and his wife were engaged, as he thought, in a quarrel, which was quite common with them, and he heard the deceased cry out 'Don't murder me. Don't kill me,' and immediately he heard a violent blow or kick given, which was quickly followed by groans. Soon after he heard a dragging along the floor, and something falling down stairs like a dead weight, when he heard the boy exclaim, 'Oh you'll kill my mother,' and then the prisoner gave a violent stamp with his foot, and said something which he did not catch.*

He also heard the same dead weight being dragged back up the stairs.

Walker was not the only neighbour to have become rather used to the Donahoos' domestic disputes. Hannah Waring, who lived opposite the Donahoos testified that '... between one and two o'clock, hearing the deceased cry out, she opened her door, and through the window of the prisoner's house saw him cross the floor towards the fire, and then she heard the deceased cry out "Thomas, don't murder me." She then went in and shut the door.'

Similarly, William Tyson, who was staying with James Walker, reported that he had heard what he described as a 'drunge' – the sound of some heavy body falling down the stairs.

By 6.30 the following morning, Donahoo was round at the Tysons' house telling them that his wife had fallen down the stairs and that he thought she was dead. 'We had a tremendous rough night last night,' said Donahoo euphemistically, 'I dare say you would hear us.' He then asked Tyson to go back next door and, showing him Ellen's body, asked him if he thought she was dead. 'Dead enough,' replied William Tyson.

If the evidence from Donahoo's son had been convincing at the inquest, it was to prove less so in the Crown Court. His story now ran that he had been awoken by a noise:

.... I got up and ran about halfway down stairs. My mother was sitting on the floor. My father was beating her. She was sitting near the pantry door. He struck her both with his hands and his feet. He had boots on. I came down stairs. My mother went on her hands and knees into the back pantry. I was standing on the floor of the house. My father told me to 'lake' the billhook. I told him I did not know where the billhook was. He got a knife, and told me he would run it through me if I did not find it. I said I could not. My father followed my mother into the pantry. He pushed open the door and got her by the hair of the head. He was drawing her out and he found the billhook. I ran up the stairs and stood there. My father put her head on his knee and lifted the billhook. I then ran up to the top of the stairs. I heard my father say it might bring him into danger, and he threw the billhook down. I then came downstairs. My father had laid my mother out on the floor. He kicked her. He told me to take her upstairs to bed. I took her by the hand and helped her up. She walked as well as she could. He followed us with a candle and a strap ...He took up her clothes and licked her with the strap; he kicked her on the shoulder. He afterwards went downstairs and told me to bring down my little sister. Before that, my father had gone downstairs and brought up a piece of wood and broke it over her, beating her ... I was wakened in the morning by my father calling 'Nellie, get up!' My mother did not speak. My father lifted her up and her head fell on one side. Some black stuff ran from her mouth. He said she was dead. I began to cry, and he told me not to cry or people might think he had done something to her. He washed her cap and her face.... He told me to say she had fallen down stairs and that he had carried her up again, and that he went to look for a bit of candle and that she fell down stairs again while he was out.

This was now James Donahoo's third version of the events of that night. Originally he had told police that his mother had fallen down the stairs. Now there was a new piece of evidence – the billhook – and a rather confused tale of what had happened.

It's hardly surprising that his story kept on changing as he must have been afraid not only of his father's vicious temper but also of the authorities. When his father was arrested, young James was also taken to the lock-up in Ulverston. Here he was told that unless he told the truth about what his father had done to his mother, his mother's ghost would come back to haunt him. He could also go back home if he told them what they wanted to know. Whether his new version was simply a fuller account of the night or a distorted version given under pressure to help gain a conviction is open to conjecture.

However, if we are to believe the surgeon's account of Ellen Donahoo's injuries, we must conclude that Donahoo had hit Ellen several times with an iron bar, shattering her skull, had kicked her in the head, breaking her jaw and thrown her down the stairs.

The jury, after less than an hour's deliberation, brought in a verdict of manslaughter. They must have believed that the 'sound of the body falling', which had been reported by the next-door neighbours William Tyson and James Walker, threw some doubt on the evidence that Donahoo had kicked his wife or battered her with the iron bar. Similarly, the evidence from James Donahoo, the son, that he had been pressurised into changing his original version of the story must also have carried some weight. To the jury, the evidence must have been too inconclusive to return a verdict of murder. The judge, however, had little sympathy. In an age when manslaughter often carried a comparatively minor punishment, he sentenced Donahoo to transportation for life.

Chapter 11

The Old Hutton Matricide 1845

I t seemed like a cut-and-dried case. Richard Simpson had killed his mother. He beat her insensible and left her to die. There were plenty of witnesses to what went on and his various versions of the story would all fail to hold water. The coroner's inquest decided on a verdict of wilful murder by Richard Simpson, but at his trial at Westmorland Assizes in August 1845, he was found not guilty.

Richard Simpson lived at Middleshaw Head, at Old Hutton, a village just a few miles outside Kendal. A widower, whose wife had died about a year earlier, he shared the house with his mother, Elizabeth, his two sons Richard and Thomas, and his sister also called Elizabeth. According to *The Times*, the house was

> ... *of the superior class of farm-houses, standing on about 36 acres of excellent land, and in a most picturesque part of the country. The house is handsomely furnished, but, from the dissipated habits of the wretched man* [Simpson], *in a state of dirt and disorder.*

Middleshaw Head was a house fuelled by alcohol and mutual hatred. According to various reports, his father (already dead at the time of the killing) was a well-known inebriate, his mother liked a tipple, his sister too found solace in the bottle, and Simpson himself was a brutal drunkard. Elizabeth Airey, the seventeen-year-old servant girl who had the misfortune of working for the Simpsons, later said at the trial at Westmorland Assizes, that Mrs Simpson was '...often ill from drink and was always telling her son that she was going to die'.

Elizabeth Simpson (the younger, Richard Simpson's sister) also had a reputation. Several witnesses, including the servants described her as being insane. Margaret Faulkner, a neighbour, said at the trial 'I think (she) is given to liquor. I have seen her appear like a drunken woman. I never saw her do anything in the household affairs.'

They also described Richard Simpson as being an impossible man, especially when drinking, who had a vile temper and reserved his greatest wrath for his mother. Mrs Simpson owned some property and it would seem that Richard hoped to inherit it on her death. He spent a great deal of time willing her dead so that he could inherit (as the eldest son) and feared that she might at any stage write a will that would exclude him. John Fenton, who had been a servant on the Simpson farm for three years, told the inquest that Simpson was in the habit of drinking to excess. He also reckoned that Simpson was in the habit of abusing his mother whenever he had been drinking.

Several of the witnesses at the inquest and his trial at Westmorland Assizes in Appleby testified that Simpson's behaviour veered between bizarre and brutal. A friend of his, John Ewan who also lived at Old Hutton, had seen Simpson at Kendal market a few weeks before the killing. He'd tried to conduct some business with him, but Simpson was so drunk he was babbling incoherently. Another friend, Edward Nelson, who had known Richard Simpson for twenty years recounted how he had often seen Simpson get drunk and that when he was in his cups, he would imagine that he was taking part in trotting races, playing the part of a horse. At other times, he threaten to shoot people.

When drunk, he was capable of anything. On one occasion, later reported by Margaret Faulkner, he had been out to Kirkby Lonsdale. Here he removed all his clothes before returning naked on horseback all the way along the turnpike. He also once told her that he'd come across the body of a young lady, but there was no truth whatsoever in it. The whole story was a product of Simpson's peculiar imagination.

On several occasions, Simpson woke John Fenton in the night and made him get up out of bed and take a loaded gun to search the house from top to bottom. Fenton could never see any explanation why he had to do this. Simpson also had the habit of waking up his young sons in the middle of the night for no apparent reason, especially when he had been drinking. Dr Longmire, one of the two doctors who carried out the post-mortem on Mrs Simpson, had treated Simpson for delirium tremens. Longmire advised him to cut down on his drinking and just stick to wine!

In a further incident, Simpson fell off his horse and, if his behaviour had been bizarre beforehand, certainly took on new twists. He imagined that his head was constantly surrounded by a swarm of bees and went reeling out into the fields, flailing at his own head in an effort to get rid of them.

Whilst some of his antics might have been amusing, or at worst bemusing, there was a sinister side to his drinking. One of the things that he did regularly when drunk was to beat his mother.

It seems that, like most of the rest of the family, Elizabeth Simpson too liked a drink. After one beating by her son, she drank only watered-down rum for a week. It was in early 1845, that Richard Simpson began beating his mother so badly that she would eventually die, which would have been handy for him, as he was heir to his mother's property.

Elizabeth Airey, the servant girl told the inquest, held at Middleshaw Head itself, how Richard Simpson had returned home from Kendal market the week before he killed Mrs Simpson between five and six in the evening. He had been drinking in Kendal all day, and it would seem that Mrs Simpson was already suffering from a beating he had previously meted out. When he eventually killed her, it would be with at least the third severe thrashing that he had given her. Elizabeth Airey's testimony was reported in *The Times* on 10 April 1845:

His [Simpson's] *mother, the deceased was in bed in the parlour. He went into the room where she was in bed, and seized her, and threw her out of bed. He asked her if she was going to get up and she said she could not bide up. She was then unwell. She had also some wounds on her, which her son Richard had done. He had abused her, kicked her, and struck her before this. On last Saturday night but one, after having dragged her out of bed, he struck her violently with the poker upon her head and upon her back. She called out for help, and I went to them, but Richard Simpson threatened to knock me down if I went near. I begged him not to strike her, but I afterwards saw Richard Simpson strike her with the poker several times over the shoulders. She cried out bitterly for help and begged me to fetch someone. I went out in search of someone, and left him beating his mother with the poker. I came back not having been able to find anyone. Mrs Simpson was lying on the floor, senseless and appeared like a dead person. Blood was flowing from her head and ears. About an hour and a half after, the servant man [John Fenton] came in. I told him what Richard Simpson had been doing to his mother. I had been into the room where my mistress was before the servant man came in, and I found the poker broken in two pieces, lying beside Mrs Simpson's head. I took the poker, and hid it in the best room. The servant man and I raised Mrs Simpson from the floor and laid her on the bed. She was insensible.*

After this pounding, Mrs Simpson became sicker still. She spent all week in bed, not taking any food, sustained only by small amounts of rum and water given to her by Elizabeth Airey. On 5 April, Simpson came home from the market in his usual state of market day intoxication. He went into his mother's room, where she was lying in bed and asked her if she was going to get up. She said she couldn't. He then asked her if she was going to give him some money and if she refused, he would go and get his gun and shoot her. When she said that she didn't have any money to give him, Simpson dragged her out of bed and began beating her again.

Poor Elizabeth seems to have had to have witnessed an awful lot of violence. She was the only other person present in the house when Simpson exploded again. When she warned Simpson that if he continued beating his mother he might end up killing her, he replied 'the sooner she's out of the way the better'. Fearing for her own safety, Elizabeth Airey ran away and stayed away from the house for at least two hours before venturing back to see what had happened. She again found Mrs Simpson lying on the floor, bleeding from her head and face, incapable of speech. When she told Richard Simpson that his mother was very ill, he said 'oh, she will come round again' and gave Elizabeth some rum with which to bathe his mother's face – medicine and cleanliness revolved round drink chez Simpsons.

Mrs Simpson survived the night and died at around mid-day the following day. Simpson sent Elizabeth Airey to fetch two neighbours, Mary Scott and Margaret Faulkner, to help 'straight her out'. When he called for the joiner, John McLean, to come and measure his mother for a coffin, McLean said that he didn't realise that his mother had been poorly, to which Simpson replied that she had 'killed herself with drinking and tumbling about'.

The inquest into Mrs Simpson's death was held at Middleshaw Head. As the officials arrived, Simpson was leaving in his gig, but changed his mind and went back into the house to hear the details of the case. The first thing he did on going back into the house was to fill several decanters with spirits with which he then plied the jury.

The post-mortem revealed just how brutal Simpson had been. James Noble and William Longmire, who were both surgeons from Kendal, conducted the examination and stated:

We find on the head, on the posterior portion of the frontal bone, on the left side, an incised wound about one inch and a half in length; and about an inch backwards from this wound on the left parietal bone, there is another wound of the same extent in a transverse direction towards the ear. These wounds appear to have been made by an instrument with a sharp edge. The poker now produced is likely to have caused them. In both these wounds the scalp was divided to the bone. They appeared to have been of some days' duration. The marks on the cap which the deceased wore corresponded precisely with the wounds above described. On removing the scalp, we found on the left side of the head that the pericranium was divided to the extent of, and corresponding with, the external wounds and the skull was here laid bare. On the right side of the head we found considerable effusion or extravasation of blood, caused by some blunt instrument. We examined the dura-mater and found extensive extravasation of blood on the brain, corresponding with the wounds and bruises before-named. On the dura-mater there were several black patches, the effects of inflammation, approaching to mortification ... The body in other parts had sustained very serious injury; there were some scratches in the front of the throat which appear to have been done by the finger-nails. On the upper part of the back there was considerable discolouration caused by violence; from the lower part of the shoulder-blades, extending over the hips, on both sides, to the anus, was one continual mass of bruises – some parts were green, others black, and some in the state of mortification, more particularly near the anus, which had extended to the peritoneum. If life had not been terminated by the injuries to the head, these bruises would have ultimately caused death. The bruises on the body must have been caused by a succession of injuries, and would require great exertion to inflict them ... We attribute the death of the deceased entirely to violence.

One of the surgeons then went on to comment that he had seen the body of a prize-fighter who had been killed after a particularly brutal boxing match and that Mrs Simpson's body was far more badly bruised.

As far as the coroner was concerned,

there was not the least doubt in his mind that R. Simpson had been the cause of the death of his mother. He never in his life heard of a case so clear; and he saw no reason in the world that they should not commit the prisoner to a court of justice to be tried for his life; he thought it was decidedly their duty to do so as Englishmen.

Arrested at the scene, Simpson's only real desire seemed to be to get a few drinks in before being carted away. He went in briefly, at the insistence of a friend, to look on his mother's body, but his face was impassive and he seemed entirely incapable of emotion at this point. When his tearful young sons came out to say their goodbyes before he was driven off to Appleby Gaol, he simply turned to them and said 'Goodbye, Dick. Goodbye, Tom.' 'His demeanour throughout the two days of the inquest was that of a person wholly unconnected with the inquiry going on,' wrote *The Times* correspondent.

Indeed, even at his trial at Westmorland Assizes the following August, Simpson seemed to be entirely unaffected by what he had done. He had even pleaded not guilty, which seemed a trifle ambitious as Elizabeth Airey had pretty much seen him do the deed and witnesses queued up to testify to his cruelty and bizarre behaviour.

Indeed, it was this bizarre behaviour that would save him from the hangman's noose. At the summing-up for his defence, Richard Simpson's solicitor, Mr Wilkins, stressed that Simpson behaved so oddly quite simply because he was insane. He did not try to deny that it was through Simpson's ill-treatment that his mother had died, but that the prisoner was in an unsound state of mind when he committed the act. He was thus unable to control himself and therefore capable of killing the parent 'for whom the most tender affections would and ought to be entertained'.

Mr Wilkins argued that had Simpson premeditated the act, he would have used some other weapon – such as a stiletto and that he would also have tried to flee the crime scene, whereas Simpson made no attempt to escape, or to bolt the doors against the outside world. 'No, he leaves the doors open and quietly betakes himself to bed. He gets up next morning and goes about quite unconcerned as if nothing whatever of moment to himself had happened.' Simpson clearly had no idea what he was doing, argued Mr Wilkins, meriting his fee.

The judge too, in his summing-up, directed the jury towards a verdict of insanity. The jury took nearly two hours – a long time by the standards of the day – before they too came to the same conclusion: Richard Simpson was insane and thus not guilty of murder. They must have thought it was their duty as Englishmen to let Simpson off the hook.

As a coda, one of the two doctors who conducted the post-mortem examination was James Noble. The Governor of the House of Correction, where Simpson was remanded for a time, was a certain James Fawcett. Later the same year, James Noble would also conduct a post-mortem examination on James Fawcett. You can find out why in the next chapter …

Chapter 12

The Killing of the Governor of the House of Correction
1845

C hristopher Fawcett had followed in his father's footsteps by becoming a policeman in Kendal. His father, James Fawcett, had moved on. Now in his fiftieth year, after three years as a constable, he had become the Governor of the House of Correction in the town, a position he had held for twelve years. But James Fawcett liked to keep his hand in as a beat policeman, and was in the habit of accompanying his son when he was patrolling the night-time streets of the town.

10 October 1845 seems to have been a particularly unruly night in Kendal. Christopher Fawcett was out patrolling the streets with his father and two constables, Busher and Ellwood, when they came across several men misbehaving. These men had been in and out of the many pubs of Kendal all evening and were now causing a disturbance. Busher and Ellwood apprehended a man called O'Neill. The two Fawcetts arrested a man called Joseph Earl, but as O'Neill was causing such a disturbance and Earl seemed reasonably quiet, Christopher went off to help Busher and Ellwood.

Earl took this as his opportunity to begin kicking up his own fuss and James Fawcett had to wrestle him to the ground in an attempt to restrain him before taking him to the lock-up in the Market Place. The *Kendal Mercury* takes up the story:

> *Earl, from what we have learnt, was upon his back in the street, and Mr James Fawcett was endeavouring to handcuff him, when two brothers, named Thomas and John Robinson came up. Thomas was in a state of intoxication, but John was not the worse for anything he*

had drunk; we believe, indeed, that two glasses of ale were the utmost which he had taken that day. When Thomas Robinson, the tipsy man, came opposite to Earl (who was still on the ground) and Mr Fawcett, who was stooping over him, he stopped and addressed himself to the parties, in a language, we believe, which Mr Fawcett had a right to suppose could only proceed from one who meditated the rescue of his prisoner. He told Thomas Robinson to keep his distance, and not interfere in the business. Thomas Robinson did not pay regard to what Mr Fawcett addressed to him, but continued his attempt to interpose, and still talked foolishly and in hostile terms to the officer in the execution of his duty.

According to Christopher Fawcett, his father 'had no official staff about him to denote he was a police officer'. However, his father did seem to be carrying a shorter weapon – a 'life preserver', a short club

Highgate, Kendal, where James Fawcett lay dying after being kicked in the stomach.

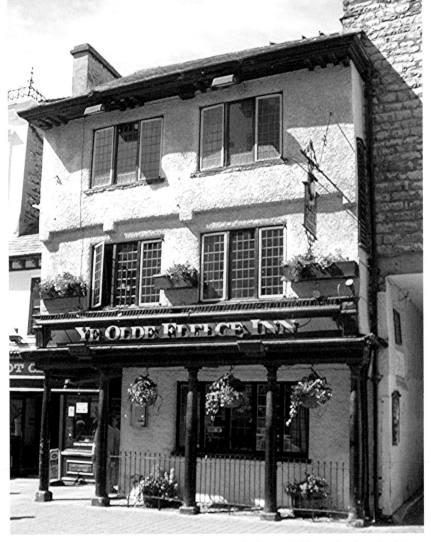

The Fleece Inn *– this is one of the pubs in which the Robinson brothers had been looking for servants on the night they became embroiled in a scuffle.*

with a lead-filled end, which could have done anyone a great deal of damage. The son later confirmed that James Fawcett was in the habit of carrying this.

As Fawcett took the life-preserver from his side pocket, John Robinson – who could not have known that Fawcett was acting as an officer of the law – chose to intervene and pull his brother away. However, Fawcett – whether accidentally or deliberately – hit John Robinson in the mouth. Robinson reeled away with two or three missing teeth and blood all over his face, before catching his breath and kicking back at Fawcett whilst Fawcett was still crouched over Earl.

Mr Fawcett instantly felt the mortal severity of the kick – he let go of Earl, and hurried to seat himself on the steps of Mrs Taylor's shop, next door to the *Angel Inn*. He said to the first person who approached him that he was 'a done man' and that 'the punch had done for him.'

As the other constables returned, Fawcett pointed out John Robinson as the man who had punched him. Robinson was immediately arrested and taken to the lock-up.

There was a light still burning in the window of the *Queen Catherine Inn* opposite. They roused the landlady, Agnes Tait, (also sometimes spelled Tate in those days of erratic spellings), who brought a glass of water for Fawcett before insisting that they take him across to her pub, where he was able to lie down. Then they sent for the local surgeon, a Mr Forrest, who bled him and gave him some sort of medicine. Whether this hastened James Fawcett's demise or not, it is impossible to tell, but it certainly didn't help. Besides, according to the *Kendal Mercury* 'the machine of life was damaged beyond the reach of human restoration'.

Fawcett's wife and eldest daughter were sent for almost immediately and when Mr Forrest returned to see his patient the following morning, it was obvious even to Fawcett that he was on his death bed. He struggled through until the afternoon, which gave him enough time to say goodbye to his wife and eight children.

The coroner's inquest took place the following Monday at Kendal Town Hall, with the Mayor, Joseph Swainson, acting as coroner. The inquest had to be delayed until the afternoon in order to allow three surgeons – Mr Forrest who had seen Fawcett on his death bed and Messrs Noble and Tatham – to examine the body. They concluded that Fawcett had died from a ruptured gall bladder and a lacerated liver, caused by the blows and kicks he'd received in the scuffle. After 'careful and protracted enquiry', the coroner passed a verdict of 'Wilful murder against John Robinson', which seems to have come as something of a shock to those people who had gathered outside the Town Hall.

John Robinson was brought in front of the Borough magistrates the next day and sent to Appleby Gaol to await trial at the Spring Assizes. He had to wait a long time by the standards of the day. Having been arrested on the night of 10 October, it wasn't until 2 April that his case was heard. By this time, the charge had been lowered to one of manslaughter on the request of the jury.

John Robinson pleaded not guilty to the charge of manslaughter. He gave the court a written statement that was intended to show that he was a decent man caught up in extraordinary circumstances. He was from a respectable family, had never been to court before, was a God-fearing Christian, had never been drunk in his life and didn't even like being out at night. The only reason he had come into Kendal and gone into the inns was that he needed to hire servants.

A number of local landowners and a clergyman were called as character witnesses for John Robinson, including a certain Thomas Fawcett, who may even have been a relative of the dead man. In fact, there were so many that Mr Ramsay, Robinson's solicitor, was able to inform the jury that there were far more people willing to speak on Robinson's behalf.

William Knipe, a farmer at Middleton, said that Robinson had lived with him for nine years and that he was 'a very peaceable, quiet man about a house as ever was. Never was in a scuffle or a bustle. Had saved money when with him. He was never but once or twice out of his bed all the time he lived with the witness and that was when away at a fair. Attended church regularly.'

The vicar, another Mr Knipe, had also known Robinson for nine years and testified that he 'saw him every day almost, and what was better saw him nearly every Sunday at church. He was the most regular, steady servant man that ever was in the neighbourhood. Never saw him either drunk or out of the way. He took part in the church music.'

In the end, the jury had little option but to find Robinson guilty of manslaughter, but they did strongly insist that the judge show clemency. In fact, Sir James Parke did exactly that. Recognising that John Robinson had spent a long time in gaol between arrest and sentence, he ordered him to pay a fine of one shilling. John Robinson was released immediately.

Fawcett had had a large family. On 7 November 1845, whilst the incident was still fresh in people's minds, the following advertisement appeared in the *Kendal Mercury* under the heading 'The Late James Fawcett's Family':

The late James Fawcett, Governor of the House of Correction, at Kendal, who lost his life in assisting the constables in the preservation of the peace, having left a widow and eight children, some of whom are young and wholly unprovided for, a subscription has been opened for the purpose of raising a fund, to be vested in trustees, and applied as occasion may require, for the benefit of the family.

Contributions to this fund are respectfully solicited, and will be received at any of the banks in Kendal.

As for James Fawcett's policeman son Christopher, the death of his father gave him a new career opportunity. By the time the trial took place, a certain Mr C Fawcett was the new governor of the House of Correction. He was following in his father's footsteps again.

There was, however, another casualty. One of the men who had helped carry Fawcett's body from the *Queen Catherine Inn* to the House of Correction was a solicitor's clerk called Luke Parker. Parker was thirty-four and originally from Manchester. Despite having a respectable job, he had a reputation as a morose drinker. He was often seen in depressed moods around the inns of Kendal and, as he drank away so much of his earnings, lived a life of near poverty.

So upset was he by the death of Fawcett, that when he carried in the body, he was babbling incoherently and said that 'it would be his turn next to be laid out'.

He went off on a drinking spree, again at the *Queen Catherine Inn*. Here, he drank himself into a near-stupor, before calling into a druggist's shop. A friend of his, who had lent him some money to buy food, saw him go in and, as Parker had a history of attempts on his own life, went in and asked what Parker had bought, which turned out to be three pennyworth of laudanum. The friend alerted Agnes Tait from the *Queen Catherine Inn*. They went out looking for Parker and when they found him, Agnes Tait tried to get him to tell her what he had taken. He denied taking anything, but went back into the *Queen Catherine Inn*, where he already had a half-finished drink. Agnes Tait watched him begin to fall asleep, nodding and dozing, and suggested that he should go home. Then, realising that he had taken laudanum, they sent for the surgeon, Edmund Tatham. Diagnosing that Parker was slipping from sleep into unconsciousness, Tatham tried to use a pump to empty Parker's stomach, but Parker couldn't be roused and slept his way into death.

Chapter 13

The Motiveless Murder of Joseph Jackson 1848

The annals of legal history are littered with bizarre versions of justice. In the nineteenth century, men were sentenced to hang on the flimsiest of evidence. However, there are instances when it is almost beyond belief that the person indicted for the crime should actually get away with it. Such was the case in the trial of Joseph Todd for the wilful murder of Joseph Jackson on 28 July 1848.

The victim was a tenant farmer. He worked a farm belonging to Mrs Youngson, near Penrith. He had done so for many years, was an established tenant of Mrs Youngson, and was well-known and, according to the newspapers of the time 'an amiable man, and much-liked by all who knew him' and a 'trustworthy person'. His cottage was on the other side of the yard from the Manor House and there would have been constant comings-and-goings as farmers, servants and family went about their duties.

Joseph Todd was employed by Mrs Youngson to look after the woods on her estate and also to act as a gamekeeper. Todd lodged with Joseph Jackson and had a room that was slightly separate from the rest of the bedrooms, accessed using a staircase leading off from the back kitchen. In this room, Todd kept some of the tools of his trade, including a single-barrelled and a double-barrelled shot-gun.

At the time of Joseph Jackson's murder, Mrs Youngson was away, and so Joseph Jackson was left to keep an eye on the general running of her estate, which was Mrs Youngson's normal practice when she had to be elsewhere. The main farm was important enough to be able to retain two domestic servants, Elizabeth Dobson, who was the housemaid, and Elizabeth Pearson, the cook.

The evening before the murder, at around ten o'clock, a certain Mr Nicholson, who had something of a reputation as a poacher, was seen in the farmyard talking to Joseph Jackson. At one o'clock that morning, everyone in both houses heard a shot. When Joseph Jackson went out the next morning, one of the gates that had been firmly shut the night before was now open. Joseph Jackson asked around the two households what they made of the shot and, when he and Todd had breakfast together with the rest of the Jackson family, he mentioned that Elizabeth Dobson had assumed that Todd was responsible. For whatever reason, this prompted Todd to go up to his room and load his gun.

Later that same day, at dinner, Joseph Todd leant over the table and said to Mrs Jackson 'There's no getting into your house for your master is always walking about.' He then walked out of the house and was not seen again until just before the shot was fired, when, with his jacket removed and his sleeves rolled up, he 'came towards his house … rather wildly, and seemed as if he had been drinking'. On his way, he passed Joseph Jackson, who was helping a local man called Carruthers, load a cart. As Joseph Todd passed them in the yard, Carruthers thought he said something about being careful not to load the cart too heavily. Todd then went into the house through the back kitchen, past Mrs Jackson who was busy washing up at the sink, down the passageway which lead to both his bedroom and the main kitchen and into the main kitchen.

In the main kitchen, the two servants from the big house, Elizabeth Dobson and Elizabeth Pearson were sitting at the table along with the Jacksons' married daughter, a Mrs Lutenor and another daughter, Mary.

Todd grabbed Elizabeth Dobson by the throat and threw her onto the floor, flung himself onto his knees alongside her and did his best to throttle the life out of the poor girl. Eventually, Mrs Jackson managed to prise him off and Elizabeth Dobson and the other servant, Elizabeth Pearson, ran off back across the yard to the Manor House.

Mrs Jackson and her two daughters did their best to calm Todd, sitting him on the windowsill and talking gently to him. For a while it looked like he was more himself, then he sprang to his feet, swearing at the women and threatening to do all sorts of mischief to Elizabeth Dobson. He stormed off down the passageway and at that point, they all feared that he had gone for one of his guns.

Mrs Jackson fled through the passageway, out of the back kitchen and across the garden to the yard, where her husband and Mr Carruthers were loading the cart to warn them that Todd was on his way with his gun. Seeing no real danger, and assuming that he could pacify his lodger, he went into the house, where he encountered Todd in the passage serving the two kitchens and Todd's bedroom.

Todd was carrying his favoured double-barrelled shotgun and Joseph Jackson tried to block the doorway with his arm and said 'Todd, what are you going to do?'

'Let me go,' shouted Todd. 'I will shoot the faggot before I rest.' (Faggot being derogatory, but not having the modern sense of the insult, was a slur aimed at Elizabeth Dobson.)

'Give me the gun,' said Jackson.

Todd stepped backwards down the passage-way and raised his gun, pointing it directly at Joseph Jackson. As he did so, the gun went off.

The shot hit Joseph Jackson in the left-hand side of his chest. Jackson staggered back down the steps, through the back kitchen and into the garden, where he collapsed. He was dead.

Carruthers ran into the house into the main kitchen and found a bewildered Todd. The gun, still smoking, was propped against the kitchen wall.

'Oh, Joe, you've shot him dead,' Carruthers said.

Todd, crying 'Oh, Joseph, oh, Joseph,' went back out into the garden, where he lifted up Joseph Jackson's hand to see if there was any sign of life. On realising what he'd done, Todd then went across the yard to the Manor House and began hammering at the door, shouting out to Elizabeth Dobson 'Oh Betty, open the door. What have I done?'

Not getting any answer, he went over to the barn and slumped on the floor. Here, Carruthers and two neighbours, Mr Collins and his son, who had by now been alerted to what was going on, tied up Joseph Todd until the constable arrived to arrest him.

He appeared at the Cumberland Assizes within a fortnight of the incident. Despite all the evidence weighing against him and the testimony of all who had witnessed the incident, the jury was somehow persuaded to bring in a verdict of not guilty. According to the *Westmorland Gazette*, the defending solicitor, Mr Wilkins, pointed out:

> *... that there was no motive whatever to induce the prisoner to injure a hair of the head of the deceased, and they could not on their consciences convict the prisoner, seeing that the gun might have gone off by accident ... in the state of agitation and anger in which he was against Elizabeth Dobson, drawing it back to prevent the deceased getting hold of it. If the hammer had caught in his dress and been partially raised it would be quite sufficient to cause the charge to explode.*

Joseph Todd was lucky; somehow the jury went for Mr Wilkins' defence. He could easily have hanged, or if the court had decided on a manslaughter verdict, been imprisoned for several years. If he didn't get away with murder, he certainly got away with manslaughter. And, if at best, we can say that he shot Joseph Jackson accidentally (which admittedly did stop Todd in his tracks), what would have happened if Jackson had not stepped into the corridor? Surely, Todd would have been across the yard and into the Manor House and possibly killed Elizabeth Dobson instead.

Todd's behaviour that day was strange. From what he said and did, one can only assume that something had sparked off his madness. The most likely explanation would be that he was paying court to Elizabeth Dobson and that he had become jealous of Nicholson, the poacher. However, Elizabeth Dobson told the court that 'Nicholson had not been paying her addresses, and that nothing had ever passed between her and the prisoner [Joseph Todd] but the most ordinary civility.'

My pet hypothesis is that Todd had developed some kind of obsession for Elizabeth Dobson. Whilst she saw nothing in their relationship, he read into everything that she said to him a significance that her actions didn't have. In the same way that stalkers come to believe that their victims are signalling to them through the drawing of curtains, for instance, Todd had developed in his mind the notion that he and Elizabeth had some kind of romantic relationship. Nicholson, who probably also upset him by poaching on the very land where Todd was supposed to be looking after the birds, had somehow done something that provoked this bizarre reaction. Todd's obsession, by the sound of it, fuelled by alcohol would then have been real enough for him. In modern parlance, Todd's condition would be described as some kind of psychosexual obsession. This is, of course, conjecture – but there's no harm in that!

Chapter 14

The Beckhouse Farm Murder 1860

Instead of being just another ordinary day in the life of a small farmer, 26 March 1860 was to prove rather unpleasant for Elizabeth Fearon. It was even worse for her poor servant girl, Ann Sewell, who wouldn't make it till sunset.

It had been a long day at Cockermouth market and Elizabeth Fearon was tired and weighed down with the goods she'd bought that day. The last thing she needed when she got home, to Beckhouse Farm in the Vale of Embleton, near Cockermouth, was to find that she was locked out of her own house.

Beckhouse was, according to the *Carlisle Patriot*,

> *...a cluster of half-a-dozen farm-houses ... situated in the Vale of Embleton, one of those beautiful avenues by which tourists annually find their way to the picturesque villages and sublime mountain passes of the Lake District. The Vale of Embleton is a secluded spot ...and ... as the traveller enters it from Cockermouth, he catches glimpses of Bassenthwaite Lake and the hills which skirt the margin of that somewhat gloomy Lake... the most prominent farmhouse is that of Mr Thomas Fearon ...*

... and now Thomas Fearon's mother was standing there, locked out.

It was early evening and there was no sign of anyone around. Presumably, Ann Sewell, whom the Fearons had employed at the Cockermouth hiring fair the previous November, was out in the fields somewhere. Mrs Fearon went out across her farmland, calling Ann's name. No reply. Still unable to get into the house and now rather fractious, she went to the next farm, owned by the Boyes family, where she enlisted the help of a servant, Sarah Earle, who was more agile than the older woman and therefore able to climb in through a window.

Sarah duly did as she was asked, but was back moments later. The sight that met Sarah's eyes could hardly have been less pleasant. Below the lobby step was the prostrate body of Ann Sewell, blood puddled around her, obviously dead.

Poor Sarah was so shocked that she backed back out of the window she'd gone in by, crying 'She's dead!' In her panic, she forgot to unlock the door to allow Mrs Fearon into the house. Mrs Fearon knew that Ann suffered from occasional bouts of fainting (it may be that Ann was epileptic) - and didn't entirely believe Sarah, who then ran off into the fields to fetch Ann's 'partner servant', George Cass.

George Cass had been hired at the same time as Ann. The idea behind 'partner servants' was that the woman would do the 'female', domestic chores and lighter duties, whilst the man would work as a labourer. He was one of three labourers on the farm, the other two being James Eland and James Boak.

Cass was on horseback and galloped to the farm, well in advance of Sarah. The door was still locked from the outside, but Cass had

Beckhouse Farm, where Ann Sewell was killed.

a little trick that he used for getting back in on nights when he was out drinking. He took an iron bar from the eaves of the house and levered the door. By this time, the Boyes's servant, Joseph Clarke, had also arrived.

Once inside, Cass could go no further, not daring to look at the body, so Joseph Clarke brushed past him and went further into the house to investigate. He found Ann, lying as Sarah had said, in a pool of blood, with her arms folded and trapped beneath her, a bloody knife in her left hand. They carried Ann's body through into the parlour (no scene-of-crime in those days!) and George Cass was sent to fetch the coroner and to go to the police.

To begin with, it was assumed that the girl had killed herself. Despite the fact that Ann's reputation was sound (even if she was known to be something of a flirt), rumours began to spread that she had fallen pregnant and had killed herself for shame. However, it soon became obvious to even an untrained eye that she had not died at her own hand, let alone her own left hand. The knife was blunt and its blade turned the wrong way, and the coroner later categorically ruled out both pregnancy and suicide.

Suspicion fell first on a young miner from Seaton called James Farrish, who had been courting Ann for six months from the time she had been in her previous employment at Camerton Hall, also near Cockermouth. Tongues wagged that there was something amiss between the two and that he had killed her in a quarrel, but alibi witnesses placed him at the mine at Green Gill. The police then had misgivings about George Cass and James Eland. Both of them had reputations for not being completely law-abiding. The day after Ann's death two local doctors, Dodgson and Williamson, carried out a post-mortem on her body upstairs at Beckhouse Farm, whilst police questioned Cass downstairs. He was referred to as being 'dull of mind' and the police set about interviewing him frequently in the hope that he would soon incriminate himself, especially as he had repeated his display of how he used the iron bar to get into the house for their benefit. As he was doing this, the two doctors pronounced that it was definitely a case of murder.

Whilst George Cass was the police's prime suspect, they still hadn't ruled James Eland out of the enquiry either. Both would later be arrested. Eland had been sharpening tools that afternoon, including a billhook – it was possible that this might have been the weapon used on Ann.

The inquest was held the following week, again at Beckhouse Farm. It was to do Cass's reputation little good as a picture was built up of a man who cared little for anyone but himself and drink.

Sarah Earle, the maid from the neighbouring farm who had found Ann's body, related several incidents that reflected badly on Cass. On the day of Ann's death, Cass had been visited by a young woman called Jane Atkinson, who had walked all the way over from Whitehaven with her young baby. Cass was the father and had not kept up payments to the poor woman. Jane Atkinson had been furious with him as he had no money and had had the cheek to send her off into Cockermouth to try to get an advance on his wages off his employer, Thomas Fearon. If that was how Cass treated women, how might he have treated Ann?

The second incident Sarah Earle related was how Ann had been frightened by a drunken Cass 'I was sure he would strike me' – although he didn't. Apart from these two incidents, Ann doesn't seem to have complained much to her friend about Cass.

Sarah also told of how she'd been sent by the Boyes, her employers, to ask Cass the whereabouts of some sheep pens on the afternoon of the murder. She reported that at that stage Cass seemed almost unable to speak, although she had not thought about it until later.

The various workers swore that they could not have been out of one another's sight for more than half an hour, then came testimony that meant that both Cass and Eland could have had the time in which to kill Ann Sewell. Mr Boyes had seen Eland coming from the house, carrying something above his head, wrapped in straw at around three o'clock on the day in question. The horse that Cass had been using that afternoon was in the stable when a certain Mr Robinson came to call, so Cass's alibi of being with the horse in the fields was shaky.

The evidence began to mount up. The hearth where Ann was found was uncleaned, but there was a pot of black lead and a brush waiting there to be used. Who would prepare to do a job and then commit suicide? There was also the fact that Cass had already said that the knife looked too blunt to do the job and that she must have had her throat slit by a billhook, which seemed a strange comment to make, especially given that there was any number of potential weapons around the farm and the farmhouse. And Eland had been sharpening a billhook that day.

Similarly, Cass made sure that he was properly cleaned up before being interviewed for the first time by police because he thought there would be blood on him as he had, in his own words 'been skinning a ewe'.

Then there was the matter of Ann's half-crown. Ann was a prudent girl who saved her money as far as possible. She had mentioned to her friend Elizabeth Hetherington, who worked at the *Bluebell Inn* that she had lost a half-crown and then found it again. Yet, there was no such coin amongst her possessions.

Moreover, Ann had seemed in high spirits that day. She had spent the morning preparing a large lunch for George Cass, the other two labourers, James Eland and James Boak, and a group of five men who had been sent over from Keswick to collect corn that Fearon had sold to their employer.

6 April 1860 was a Good Friday, but not for Eland and Cass. They were both arrested and Cass was taken to the gaol in Cockermouth for questioning, whilst Eland was taken to Higham Hall.

Immediately, Cass began to spill out a confession in which an argument between Ann Sewell and him had developed into a slanging match. She'd then thrown a knife at him, grazing his cheek and that's when he'd lost his temper completely. After the murder, he then took her money from her room upstairs. It was a lengthy confession that Cass dictated line-by-line allowing the clerk, a Mr Musgrave, time to finish writing one sentence, before moving onto the next. Eland was released without charge.

On 14 April 1860, Cass was charged with the wilful murder of Ann Sewell and was tried at the Midsummer Assizes in Carlisle in the August. By this time, he changed his mind about his confession (he'd made another by this stage), withdrawing all previous statements and pleading not guilty. However, the weight of all the

Higham Hall – now a residential adult education college. James Eland was taken here for questioning into the murder of Ann Sewell.

evidence was against him, as was the flimsiness of his alternative story – that he'd met a man with a billhook coming from the direction of the farmhouse on the day of the killing.

In gaol, awaiting execution, Cass then made the third of his confessions.

> *I was smoking my pipe after dinner and, about 3 o'clock, Ann Sewell began to call me ugly names and taunted me about my bastard child. She said everybody hated me. She then threw some cinders out of the grate. I jumped up and got hold of a knife that was on the table. I got hold of her by the shoulder and cut her throat. After I saw the blood I wished I had not done it. I thought I could not mend it so I cut her throat again.*

As ever, the Victorian crowds were out in force: they loved nothing more than a good hanging. There hadn't been one in Carlisle for five years, so the locals were looking forward to this. Indeed, the thought of large numbers of people thronging the streets of the County Town so worried the authorities that they debated rescheduling it for 7.00 in the morning to beat the crowds. However, the High Sheriff wouldn't countenance moving the execution from its midday slot; a man was having his life foreshortened, it was not in his gift to foreshorten it even further. In response, so as to divert the crowds elsewhere, the local authorities laid on cheap day trips by train to nearby Silloth so that people could enjoy a breath of sea air instead.

The day trips didn't attract much business. The hanging of George Cass pulled in a crowd of 4,000 with people, including Ann's sweetheart James Farrish, using the trains to get into Carlisle to see the execution. For many people, it was a good family day-out. Youngsters were hoisted onto shoulders or climbed statues and walls to get a better view.

The hangman for the day was William Calcraft. It was Calcraft's public execution of Martha Brown in Dorchester in 1856, witnessed by a sixteen-year-old Thomas Hardy, that was eventually to become the inspiration for *Tess of the D'Urbevilles*. He was the official hangman for Newgate Prison, where he also carried out any floggings that were needed. Even in those days he was on a weekly retainer of a guinea (£1.05, worth probably around £600 compared with today's wages). Each time he hanged anyone at Newgate, he got another guinea, although floggings were a more niggardly half-crown (12½ p). When Calcraft could really make some money was when he went off to other gaols, such as Carlisle, when he could charge anything from £10 to £15 (c.£6,000-9,000 when compared with today's wages). As with many hangmen, there were also useful little additional sources of income. The executioner was, by law, allowed to keep the clothes in which a prisoner was hanged and could also sell the body for dissection. When Calcraft hanged the notorious Staffordshire serial killer, Dr William Palmer, who had killed around fourteen people, but who hanged for only one murder, Palmer dressed deliberately in prison garb so as to make his clothes worthless. Calcraft got his revenge, though. He sold off small sections of 'the rope that hanged Palmer' at inflated prices to ghoulish souvenir hunters. Rumour has it that there was far more rope sold off than ever went round Palmer's neck! The story also goes that as he mounted the scaffold, it swayed under his considerable bulk and Palmer asked Calcraft 'Is this thing safe?' - a genuine example of gallows humour. Cass would have been neither intellectually capable of such a remark, nor was he likely to, as he was fighting back tears.

Like many killings, Cass's murder of Ann Sewell, would seem to be something that happened on the spur of the moment. Although a couple of witnesses testified that they had heard Cass threaten to kill the girl, it is likely these were invented to ensure he hanged or just idle talk from a man with a violent temper.

None of this would have happened had it not been for the hiring fair in Cockermouth where the Fearons chose Ann. In the nineteenth century, it was

Ann Sewell's headstone, St Cuthbert's church, Embleton.

common practice for farmers to hire servants and agricultural labourers at such events. Whilst there may have been something of the cattle-market about such a day, it was the custom. Poor Ann, who would have been there in all good faith, couldn't have realised that this was going to lead to her death when she was taken on by the Fearons to work alongside George Cass.

Her short stint as a maid at Cockermouth would have ended that summer. As it is, she is still in Embleton, buried in St Cuthbert's churchyard. Her funeral took place on the Thursday after her murder and the church was packed. Amongst those gathered to pay their respects to Ann was the man who was later to be convicted of her murder, George Cass. He is reported to have said, 'Who'd have thought Sewell would have gone so soon, poor thing?'

Often in such cases, the evidence provided would not stand up to modern scrutiny. However, in this particular case, given the fact that Cass made a final confession when he no longer needed to, it is probable that he was the murderer. True, there are people who will confess to crimes they haven't committed, but given the other pieces of circumstantial evidence and Cass's known poor treatment of women, we must guess that Ann Sewell spurned his advances, perhaps having teased him a little too much. Being 'dull of mind', perhaps Cass was unable to differentiate between flirting and sexual invitation.

In the churchyard at Embleton, Ann Sewell's tombstone reads simply 'In memory of Ann Sewell, whose life was terminated by the hand of an assassin whilst in the discharge of her humble duty on the 26th day of March 1860, died aged 26 years'.

Chapter 15

A Trades Union Murder
1865

W orking and living conditions in the nineteenth century often ran the gamut from poor to atrocious. Save for those few workers with more enlightened – if paternalistic – employers, life for most urban workers was harsh. Pay was poor and many had to eke out a hand-to-mouth existence, not helped by the fact that the temptation to drink away the misery of such a life tended to worsen the situation.

In such a climate, the need for workers to band together into Trades Unions in order to apply pressure on employers was seen by many as so important, that those who wouldn't join in the cause were often treated badly by their colleagues. Rows were common and fights not unheard of, but rarely did violence escalate to such an extent that anyone would be killed.

For one poor unfortunate, William Blackburn, a bricklayer from Barrow-in-Furness, his refusal to join in Union activities led to his death. In those days, Barrow was rapidly developing from a tiny fishing village into a powerhouse of the Victorian maritime economy. The *Manchester Courier* even went so far as to describe it as 'the rising town of Barrow-in-Furness near Ulverstone (sic)'.

William Blackburn was described by the press of the day as a 'quiet, inoffensive man' and by the doctor who knew his family as 'an exceedingly funny man, and used to be a comic singer'. He had belonged to his local trade union for twenty-three years, since starting work as a ten-year-old, but when he tried to renew his subscription and sent in his 2s 6d (12½ pence), his fellow unionists refused to accept it as they deemed him to be working 'black' – in other words, he had been working with non-union labour.

It was not enough for his fellow unionists to turn down his membership; they also started to jeer at him in the street. Then, a

Devonshire Dock Hall – the modern dockyard - from above the roof-tops of Barrow-in-Furness. Several of the men involved in the killing of William Blackburn were employed in the yards that once stood here.

gun was fired outside the door of his house behind George Street. The name-calling and insults began to rise to a pitch until matters came to a tragic conclusion on Sunday, 22 October 1865.

Blackburn had been at home with his wife and some friends having a drink and, because he was due to work an extended shift the next day, decided to chop the wood for the following evening's fire that night. As was his habit, he popped down the road to some friends, the Kenyons who lived a few doors away, to borrow an axe to chop firewood. On his way back to his house, he was stopped in the street by a group of men. What followed next is not entirely clear, but the axe was taken off him and used against him.

According to Blackburn's wife, Louisa, when she heard the rumpus outside, she went into the street to find him. Her testimony to the inquest ran:

> *I heard my husband say 'Oh, Louisa, I am near killed!' I said 'Whatever are you doing here?' Harry Waites I found was near the place, and said, 'It serves him right, but it's not me that's done it.' My husband was sitting just within Waites's yard, with his face towards our street, and trying to get up. He was sitting between a large stone and the yard wall. Waites's servant was standing at their own back door, with a candle in her hand* [this would be Margaret Hargreaves], *and there were three or four men with her. They never*

spoke, and I said they ought to have had better sense than to take advantage of a man who had a sup of drink.

Louisa Blackburn immediately sent for Dr Stevenson, who arrived with a policeman. Dr Stevenson sewed up Blackburn's head wound and the injured man was put to bed, where he later died.

As soon as he heard that Blackburn was dead, one of the men involved in the scuffle, William Lawson, came forward and confessed to his part in the crime. Eventually, several other men were arrested, but there was so much confusion as to what happened that the authorities had trouble getting at the truth. It seemed that those most involved in the crime were Henry Waites and three men who lodged in his house – William Lawson, Alexander (Sandy) Wallace and James Garlick.

It's extremely difficult to unravel exactly what took place as the witnesses' statements were at such variance with one another. They couldn't all agree as to who started the scuffle that was to lead to Blackburn's death, nor even on whether Blackburn was drunk or not. He had certainly been drinking. In fact, he had drunk steadily all day, but his wife described him as being 'fresh', which would probably translate as somewhere around the 'half-cut' mark in modern parlance – in other words, he wouldn't have passed a breathalyser test, but nor would he have been staggering around wildly. In an era when drinking was often extraordinarily heavy, being in a state like this was probably far from unusual. Amongst the six people gathered at the Blackburns' house they had consumed two quarts of ale and a gill of rum, not huge quantities by the standards of the day.

At the inquest, Margaret Hargreaves, who was a servant to Henry Waites – the accused man who ran the corner shop - said that she had not been able to stand next to Blackburn shortly before the incident as he smelled so strongly of rum. However, Margaret was not the world's most reliable witness. Later, at the Assizes, she testified that she was in Waites's kitchen shortly after the scuffle, where all the men were talking. Margaret repeatedly denied knowing what the men were talking about because she was reading her bible – an impressive feat for someone who when asked to give a sample of her reading in court, proved to be completely illiterate.

John Willan, a carter, testified that whist he was talking to Margaret Hargreaves they had seen a man who was obviously very drunk – by inference William Blackburn – remonstrating with another man, accusing him of listening at his door. He admitted that although he didn't really see it all, he had witnessed Blackburn threaten the others with whatever it was he was carrying and that someone – possibly the man with the Scottish accent – had taken it off him and hit him with it, but that there was no further hitting or kicking when Blackburn fell.

The next witness, Susannah Crane, heard noises, but didn't see anything, which didn't clarify anything. Then a neighbour, Margaret Archibald, told yet another version of events. Amongst other things, she heard one voice say to Mrs Blackburn 'It served him right what he got', whilst others said 'It's a serious thing to strike with an axe,' 'Well, I've not done it' and 'I'll take the consequences of what I did'. However, she wasn't able to attribute any of these statements to any individuals and didn't hear a Scottish voice.

Henry Waites, whose servant Margaret Hargreaves had already testified that William Blackburn stank of rum, said that Blackburn had accused him of listening at his door. He also reported that Wallace had said to Blackburn 'You've got the wrong man this time', although what was meant by this was never explained.

Contrary to what was said by the Waites' household, Mrs Kenyon, who had loaned Blackburn the axe, testified that Blackburn wasn't drunk and in fact had helped her rather incapacitated husband home.

Not only was there talk of a man with a Scottish accent – importantly only amongst those who were actually involved in the scuffle itself - there was talk of a fall. Henry Waites's testimony implied that Blackburn had wielded an axe, that he and his lodgers had run away and as they did so, the drunken Blackburn fell onto a gatepost. He also reckoned that Blackburn had said 'It is entirely my own fault and if you'll forgive me, I'll beg you all pardon' – a bizarre thing to say (and, to be frank probably entirely untrue).

William Lawson then changed his story. He now reckoned that all the others were trying to put the blame on him, although he admitted he had punched Blackburn, who had then fallen head-first over a gatepost.

Later, Dr Henry Richmond Stevenson's cross-examination by the coroner meant that the possibility that Blackburn died because of a fall was dismissed. According to the report in the *Barrow Herald*, Dr. Stevenson testified that:

The skull was broken inward ... I took away a portion of the bone, and afterwards took some more pieces away. The piece I produce is the largest piece I took away. Had the blow been given with the sharp part of the axe, the wound would have been a clean cut, but it was a complete crash ... A fall from a great height upon a stone would produce such a wound, but in that case I should have expected to find dirt or earth in the wound. There was none in this case. There was a bruise on his right elbow, which, no doubt was caused by his falling down after he received the blow, but it was a mere abrasion of the skin. There were distinct marks on the abdomen as if from the sparrow-bids of a man's shoe, which must have been produced by kicks, or being stamped upon with the feet. He had vomited a quantity of blood.

Later, at the magistrates' court, William Blackburn's evidence, which had been refused by the coroner on the basis that Blackburn had not realised he was dying when he made the statement, was accepted, thereby giving the victim's version of events:

...I went to a neighbour's house to borrow an axe to cut some firewood with. I borrow it regularly, and on coming back I found the prisoner, Alexander Wallace, listening at my door. There were other persons also there. I went up to the prisoner and said 'You deserve a belt with the axe for listening at my door.' I immediately got a knock from the prisoner right over my left eye, which knocked me down. I did not see whether he had anything in his hand when he struck. The axe was taken from me by someone before I received the blow. I cannot say exactly whether I was knocked down or pulled down at first. I got several blows when I was down. I could not say that the prisoner took the axe from me. I did not know the prisoner before. I know him by his dress ... When I fell I think my head went against a barrel. The man who is at the corner shop said when I fell 'It served

him right.' The man's name is Henry Waites. I feel very ill and weak.
I have been a union man, but am not one now.

At the trial at Lancaster Assizes in the spring of 1866, Alexander Wallace was tried for feloniously killing William Blackburn. His three friends, William Lawson, Henry Waites and James Garlick were tried for aiding and abetting Wallace. Given that it was Lawson who had owned up to the deed earlier, there seems to have been a great deal of confusion on the part of the authorities as to whom they should try for what.

As a result, Lawson, Waites and Garlick were acquitted. That left Wallace – would someone be found responsible for the crime? No. When Mr Gardener, a builder from Barrow-in-Furness, spoke on behalf of Alexander Wallace and stated that he 'knew the prisoner, Wallace, to be a steady man', Wallace too was let off. The theory that William Blackburn had fallen on the stone gatepost knocked over in the yard seems to have held. Perhaps the jury felt that Blackburn's threatening behaviour with the axe had led to his own death.

It's hard not to be sceptical, even cynical about the verdict, especially considering the confession made by William Lawson. For months before, during and after the trial of the four men, the 'murder' was the talk of the town and filled the columns of local newspapers. The entire concept of Trades Unions came under severe scrutiny as correspondents to the newspapers aired both sides of the argument as to their value. No matter what the outcome, however, it didn't do the Trades Unions any favours. Whilst the Unions wanted to have the strongest possible negotiating position by trying to ensure that everyone joined, frowning on those who didn't, or who worked with non-union labour, beating a 'scab' to death is taking things to extremes.

William Blackburn left a widow and five children. Despite the polarisation of opinion in the letters column, there was huge sympathy in the town for the bereaved family. Three local men, Birchall, Wells and Kenyon, the neighbour whose axe Blackburn had borrowed, raised £16 for the widow and children and other donations poured in. Whether the local union paid anything into the fund, I haven't been able to establish.

Chapter 16

The Navvies' Punch-up 1870

There have always been rivalries when workers from one part of the country – or even a different country altogether – are drafted in to work alongside the locals. Sometimes this is just jocular and light-hearted, but if the groups are treated differently, then this often leads to resentment and occasionally boils over into something a little more physical.

One of the most notable of such incidents took place in October 1870, when workers were busy constructing what is now known as the Settle-Carlisle railway. Both English and Irish navvies were brought in to do the heavy work of constructing the track for the section of the Midland railway that would link Armathwaite with Carlisle to the North and the Dales to the South.

Armathwaite railway station – it was whilst building this stretch of what is now the Settle-Carlisle line that Cornelius Cox was battered to death in a dispute.

Whilst life for both the English and the Irish workers would have been tough, it was the Irish who had the poorer of the conditions. The English workforce lived in cottages in the village, but the Irish were forced to live in a shanty town of huts outside the village itself. Even local pubs became unofficially segregated, so the Irish navvies had essentially taken over a pub, the *New Inn*, in Armathwaite and made it their own – probably because the English didn't want to be seen drinking with them – and vice versa.

15 October 1870 was a pay day and for some reason best known to themselves, a group of around twenty English navvies decided that on that night they would take over the *New Inn* for their drinking. At around 9.00 o'clock that evening, a group of Irish labourers arrived at the pub. Finding themselves forced out of their usual watering-hole, they began to pick up stones with which they pelted the pub, smashing all the windows. Some of the English took refuge upstairs and the landlord led his own family into the cellar for safety.

In the fighting that ensued, one of the Irishmen, Cornelius Cox, was very badly injured. He was found a couple of hours after the trouble began, lying on his back in a field on the far side of the pub's six-foot wall. The police put him in a barrow and wheeled him to the hut where he lived, but Cornelius Cox died two days later.

The post-mortem that followed soon established what was obvious to even the most casual observer. Cox had a fractured skull and extensive wounds to the side of his head. Death itself was caused by a massive blood clot that had pressed on his brain.

The police arrested three Englishmen, William Kaiseley, John White and Charles Parker, who were all in their early twenties. The case was due to be heard at the Spring Assizes, but because there was no material witness to the crime, it was postponed until the Summer Circuit.

In his opening riposte to the prosecution's case, which placed the three men firmly in the frame, the defending lawyer, Mr Campbell Foster, played on the fact that there was animosity between the two sets of labourers and that all the witnesses for the prosecution were Irish.

Indeed the witnesses were to prove less than reliable. The story of one of the Irish navvies, Foster, was that he had seen John White set about Cornelius Cox whilst in the pub, knocking him down. Then, William Kaiseley and Charles Parker dragged Cox outside and whilst White and Kaiseley pinned down Cox's legs, Parker set about his head with a heavy shovel. Foster's story had a part-corroboration when another Irish navvy, a M'Donough, told a similar tale, although he stated that he couldn't see what weapon was used.

Yet, M'Donough testified that after the fracas, all four Irishmen present were then invited by Kaiseley to sit down and share a half-gallon jug of ale with their English counterparts. The defence leapt on this, arguing that it seemed entirely improbable that the two parties would sit down together when one group had just witnessed their mate's head being staved in. What's more, it was an extremely dark night and he cast doubt on the fact that Foster claimed to have actually seen all this.

The evidence was tenuous at best and in his summing-up, the judge mentioned several factors that would point the jury towards their verdict. Apparently Foster had sworn that there was no bad feeling between the two groups, yet there had obviously been trouble fomenting for some time and when two sides clash like this, one has to presume that there is some sort of ill-feeling. He also pointed out that Foster and others had looked on whilst their friend was beaten to death without raising any kind of alarm. He also pondered the question that, given the death took place during a fight, this might also be a case of manslaughter rather than murder.

The all-English jury decided that the prisoners were guilty of neither murder nor manslaughter and they were free to go, although one wonders how much this must have rankled the Irish navvies. Feelings between Irish catholic groups and the locals were poor in other areas and this was not the only case of friction on record. On 30 July 1884, under the heading 'The Orange Riots in Cumberland', *The Times* ran the following article:

Yesterday the Whitehaven magistrates continued the hearing of the case against 20 prisoners charged with rioting at Cleator Moor on July 12. Mr H. Shee appeared for the Roman Catholic prisoners.

Fifteen witnesses were examined. Mr Shee having addressed the court for his clients, Mr Paisley, of Workington, addressed the bench on behalf of the Orangemen. At a late hour in the afternoon the magistrates retired, and, on returning into court, the chairman said they dismissed the cases against Joseph Dixon, James Dunn, John Houston, Samuel Scott, Daniel Doran, James Heldon, James Mcloughlin, Patrick Madine, James Sloan, James Stafford, and Philip Waters. The first four are Orangemen, and the others Roman Catholics belonging to Cleator Moor. The bench committed for trial at the Cumberland assizes John Bawden, the leader of the Orangemen, Simon John Cordner, Workington, Henry Lavery, Whitehaven, John Moore, Distington, Orangemen; and Thomas Cain, Thomas Cavanagh, John Hannen, William M'henry, and James Ryan, Roman Catholics.

Bail was fixed in each case at £30 and two sureties of £15 each.

Nor are incidents such as these simply a by-product of the 'industrial' age. Centuries before Wordsworth romanticised the Lake District and the place began to be seen as a potential holiday destination for wealthier Britons needing to breathe fresher air than they could in the cities, the hills of England were a mineral resource. There was industry in Cumbria long before the revolution turned half of the country into a dark, satanic mill-owner's sweatshop.

In the sixteenth century, as Queen Elizabeth I girded Britannia's loins to do some wave ruling (or rule waiving, if you prefer), so money was needed to pay for the royal expeditions and the defence of the realm. Copper was needed for the production of arms as well as machinery. The potential prizes on offer were great. The Crown was entitled to 9/10ths of all gold and silver, as well as handsome rates on all other minerals.

As Britain lacked the expertise to exploit the rich copper deposits of Lakeland, Elizabeth turned to continental Europe for help, and in particular Germany. Bavaria was considered to be the area that led the world in mining techniques and the city of Augsburg, founded in Roman times, was an important financial and commercial centre. In 1564, The Society of Mines Royal was founded as a means of enticing German experts to take over the management of mining throughout the Kingdom.

Derwent Isle – following the murder of Leonard Stolz, the German miners in Elizabethan Keswick lived here for their own protection.

Thus it was that a group of miners from Augsburg, under the leadership of Daniel Hoechstetter (or Hechstetter) arrived in the valleys around Keswick in June 1564. In no time at all, they had discovered rich veins of copper in Borrowdale, which they called Barnthal, and the Newlands (Neulandt) Valley. Their most important mine soon attracted the moniker of 'Goldscope', not because they found gold in any quantity, but because the locals soon managed to corrupt the name the Germans gave the mine from 'Gottesgab' (God's gift).

The Germans brought with them technologies that were unknown to the resident Brits. They were also given more powers than some of the locals. Hoechstetter and his colleague Thurland were granted a commission to fell trees in the woodlands and the rights to 'apprehend disorderly persons', potentially a cause of some of the friction that was to come.

Although the Elizabethan age saw the High Seas opening up to an unprecedented degree, allowing larger and more exciting adventures, the ordinary person ventured little from his native area. In the Lakeland Fells, folk from neighbouring valleys were often treated with suspicion, let alone a group of comparatively wealthy 'Dutchmen' (the corruption of Deutsch), who were seen to be enjoying greater success and a wealthier lifestyle than the locals.

The Germans were well-paid, attractive to the local girls and far better miners than their English counterparts. To begin with, resentment ran high. At least one German was killed. In his letters home, Hoechstetter refers to an attack on a Leonard Stolz by an armed mob led by a man called Fisher in which Stolz died. At one point, the miners had to hole up on Derwent Isle in the middle of Derwentwater so as to have protection from the locals. After all, they were over here, taking our jobs and our women.

Indeed they were and by 1580 there had been nearly forty marriages between German miners and the local girls and, according to the late local historian George Bott, the parish registers at the local church in Crosthwaite record the births of 176 children to German fathers in the first twenty years or so of work. The Hoechstetters' daughter Susanna even married a local dignitary, Allan Nicholson of Hawkshead Hall. Eventually, the two cultures merged and you couldn't see what the problem had ever been.

I have no doubt that if you drop even further back into history, you would find stories of animosity between various nationalities. Indeed, the Border Reivers, clannish robbers, burglars, thugs and thieves robbed and killed each other for the sake of national pride in the disputed debatable lands of the English-Scottish borders in the North of Cumbria.

However, in Armathwaite, amongst the navvies building the railway, there was still one lingering, smouldering reason for friction. Not only was Cornelius Cox dead, but the justice that had been meted out afterwards was at best peremptory and, at worst, rough. However, it would be difficult to find Kaiseley, White and Parker guilty on the evidence presented. One wonders how hard the police of the day worked to find witnesses and evidence.

Chapter 17

The Unsolved Murder of
Lucy Sands
1882

On 1 March 1882 a road-mender fixing a stretch of the street near Workington Bridge Station went to fetch some small rocks from a pile lying handily on the verge. To his horror, when he removed the top layer, he found that the stones formed a small cairn covering the body of a young girl. The shoeless corpse lay with arms by its sides, head turned to the left and from the signs of decay, it was obvious that it had been there for some time.

Investigators soon worked out that the body was that of Lucy Sands. Lucy was just sixteen years old and had not been seen in the town for some months. Her grandmother, Sarah Stewart, with whom she lived was quite used to Lucy coming and going as she pleased and simply assumed that this was one of her longer jaunts away from home. She had done this before when she went off to work as a maid in Liverpool, so she thought little of it when she hadn't heard from Lucy in months. When faced with the terrible news of what had happened to her granddaughter, Sarah Stewart was almost inconsolable.

Piecing together witness statements, the police concluded that she had last been seen alive in the area on 1 December the previous year. On the evening for which they could last find any sighting of Lucy, she, together with two teenage friends, Jane Shannon and Margaret Cranney, had gone to visit the young man with whom Margaret was then 'walking out'.

The 'young man' in question was a certain Maynard James Harrison, the son of one of the managers at the West Cumberland Ironworks. It would seem that Mr Harrison was in high demand amongst the girls, possibly because he was a notch or two above

The house where Lucy Sands lived with her grandmother, who failed to report her missing.

them in social standing. Margaret was not the only one of the trio who had her heart set on Harrison. Lucy too was obviously keen on him, according to a later statement by her cousin, James Reay. At the later murder trial, he was reported by the *Maryport Advertiser* as having visited Lucy's house twice that day and:

> The first time he was in he saw Lucy curling her hair.
> He said, 'You are taking a deal of pain with yourself; what is the matter?'
> She said, 'I am going to see my young man.'
> He replied, 'Have you a young man?'
> 'Oh yes I have,' she replied.
> He asked her who he was and she replied 'They call him Mr HARRISON?' She said this twice over. She said no more, and he left her in the house.

According to the statements collected from Margaret Cranney and Jane Shannon, they had been given a tour of the works by Maynard

James Harrison, before he took them back to his parents' house, where they messed around in the garden for around quarter of an hour. At 8.45 that evening, Lucy left saying that she had to meet a lad called Billy Wilson, Margaret Cranney went a few minutes later, which left Jane Shannon alone with Maynard Harrison, until Margaret returned at about 9.30.

The presumed last sighting of Lucy Sands was by a woman called Hannah Gibson, who stated that she had seen Lucy on her own not far from Harrison's house. She gave the time as being at around nine o'clock, although there is nothing to corroborate this and it is highly doubtful that she even had any means of giving a precise time. Maynard Harrison denied seeing Lucy after she had left his parents' house shortly before nine o'clock.

It would seem, therefore, that the only other person to see Lucy Sands alive was her killer. Could it then have been Billy Wilson? Billy Wilson, a stonemason who lived nearby, was later to swear on oath at the inquest that he hadn't seen Lucy in the past week and certainly had no plans to meet her that evening. He also had alibi witnesses.

The police already had strong suspicions about Maynard Harrison. They were perturbed by the fact that Harrison could identify the colour of the girl's stockings on the night she disappeared – this is an era of full-length skirts, when 'until a man is married, he doesn't know whether his wife's knees are made of wood or not'. He was arrested even before the inquest was held, which was a case of putting a rather wobbly cart before the horse. Maynard's cause was not helped by the inquest that was held at the *Green Dragon Hotel* in Workington less than a fortnight after the road-mender's appalling discovery. It would seem that no-one had a good word for the young man.

Jane Shannon told the inquest that Harrison had asked to her to swear that she'd seen him grab Lucy by the leg whilst they were messing about in the garden. This, of course, would provide an explanation as to how he knew the colour of her stockings. Margaret Cranney, however, without prompting did admit that she'd seen Harrison spinning Lucy around.

Two former servants in the Harrison household, Alice Atkinson and Liz Smith, swore that they had seen young Harrison

Carlisle railway station – when they left the courthouse, witnesses Jane Shannon and Margaret Cranney had to run a gauntlet of insults and were smuggled onto the train here.

clambering into his bedroom via the washroom roof in the early hours of the morning following the murder.

Thomas Rosser, a tailor, who was a drinking buddy of Harrison's, also testified that Harrison had confessed to Lucy's killing whilst he was in his cups.

Maynard's inevitable remanding to the Assizes in Carlisle was compounded by further testimony in another court appearance in Workington at the end of March. Most telling of the evidence given was that of Evan Jones, a draughtsman at Distington Ironworks. According to the *Maryport Advertiser*:

> *On the 1st March last witness met the prisoner in Pow-street about twenty minutes to five o'clock in the afternoon. His aunt was with*

him at the time, and they all went into the Royal Oak.

Witness had a glass of ale and prisoner had a glass of whiskey standing on the table. Did not meet the prisoner in the street; he was standing near BOYD's, the clothier's, and the prisoner whistled to him. Prisoner asked him if he had heard about the murder, and he replied that he had. He also said it was a strange thing that the body had lain so long on the public road. Prisoner took a glass of whiskey in his right hand and winking his eye said, 'I knew where the body was long since; I knew from the first.' He said he knew Lucy SANDS and was with her the night she was missed - he was in the garden with her in company with two other girls. Witness asked prisoner if he wanted another glass, and he replied, 'No.' Prisoner said he was left with the two girls at the garden gate. His aunt was in a 'terrible way.' When prisoner made the statement to the effect that he knew where the body was she threw her hands up. Witness cautioned him to be careful what he was saying. Just as witness was leaving the Royal Oak he met two girls in the passage, and they told MAYNARD he was wanted, and he went off with them. Did not know the girls at the time, but he recognised them now as CRANNIE and SHANNON.

This was followed by other testimony. Witness after witness was called, each of whom managed to add another little twig to the fire of suspicion that had been lit under Harrison. According to them, Harrison had taken an undue interest in the case; Harrison had claimed Lucy had gone to Preston to work; Harrison had implied that Lucy had got her just desserts; Harrison had said that Lucy was a whore; Harrison had shown one witness a gun and a knife – and indeed the police did remove a gun from Harrison's house.

Some of the evidence was contradictory and the testimony of the two servant girls, who had sworn just a fortnight earlier that they had seen Harrison sneaking over the wash-house roof to get in through the bedroom window on the night of Lucy's disappearance now seemed less sure of the actual date. Nonetheless, the cart was in full motion and it was inevitable that the case was then referred to the Assizes in Carlisle. If the story had been a sensation before the trial, it was now going to take an even sharper turn. The *Maryport Advertiser* continues the story:

At the assizes at Carlisle on Wednesday the Grand Jury ignored the bill against MAYNARD JAMES HARRISON, who was charged with having murdered LUCY SANDS at the North-side, Workington on the 1st December last. This result of the proceedings against HARRISON was generally expected, and it has created very little surprise.

No petty jury could have been found to convict the prisoner upon such slender testimony as the prosecution were able to offer against him. It is quite true that he was in the company of Lucy Sands on the night when she was last seen alive, but this fact, and the statements which he has made to several persons, certainly do not constitute a chain of evidence against him as would warrant any person in assuming that he is guilty of her murder.

One would have thought that the matter of Harrison's crime would have ended there, but such was the hysteria whipped up by the murder that when Harrison was released from the courtroom and went to the *Red Lion* on Botchergate in Carlisle with friends and family, the pub was immediately surrounded by a crowd hoping for a glimpse of the man whom the public were all convinced was a murderer.

The two main witnesses – Margaret Cranney and Jane Shannon were treated even more badly, presumably because they were seen as behaving indecently. Immediately the case collapsed and they left the courtroom, they were surrounded by a mob and had to be led by the police to the safety of the police station. They were then escorted via a back passage to a house and smuggled to the railway station. According to the *Maryport Advertiser* they 'were darting about to evade the mob like rats in search of a hole'. Meanwhile, two of the other witnesses, Annie Bell and Sarah Kennedy, were mistaken for Jane Shannon and Margaret Cranney and the mob was so violent and abusive they had to take refuge in a shop.

When poor Margaret Cranney and Jane Shannon did arrive back at Workington Station, a large crowd was waiting for them and they were set upon in the street. It wasn't just insults that were thrown at them, but mud and stones and Jane Shannon was knocked to the floor. Harrison had managed to avoid the crowds by taking a carriage to Dalston and arriving home on a different train from that expected.

There is no doubt that the story of poor Lucy Sands became a morality tale about young girls not flirting and behaving in a provocative manner. Maynard James Harrison still has the stench surrounding him of being the likeliest culprit. However, a lot of that is caused by his having been so unpopular at the time of his trial. True, his story is not fully convincing and there are elements that are unexplained, but it would seem that this is one of those cases where the self-righteousness of the public got out of hand.

The moral indignation of the crowds that thronged the streets baying for his blood are not untypical of those today, who often claim some kind of higher purpose when behaving little better than the person who committed the crime itself.

It was no doubt whipped up by the local media as the *Maryport Advertiser* in its report of the acquittal of Maynard James Harrison does not paint him in the most flattering light:

> *As for HARRISON himself, no right-minded person can have any sympathy with him. He is evidently an ill-conditioned lad who prides himself upon that which he ought to be ashamed of; while -- if the statements of some of the witnesses are to be relied on -- the language which he used about the dead girl after her body was discovered was simply brutal, and proves he has a great deal to learn, and a very great deal to unlearn.*

If the story does have a moral it is that the police needed to collect solid evidence and not rely on hearsay. They acted too swiftly to try to show that Harrison was the killer with very little to link the boy to the crime. That he was acquitted was entirely correct in the circumstances. Maynard Harrison was a selfish ne'er-do-well, who liked to boast and seems to have wanted several girlfriends; that he was the murderer is not borne out by what evidence we have. There are many selfish, boastful ne'er-do-well seventeen-year-olds who would love to have several girlfriends – that doesn't automatically make them murderers.

It may be that he killed Lucy when she refused to have sex with him, but there is no evidence for this. If he killed her purely because it was in his nature to do so (which was implied at the time), then we would expect from our modern understanding of this kind of behaviour, that he would have continued to attack women. There are no reports of this. It may be that Billy Wilson's alibi was false; but again there is no evidence for this. In other words, any possible conclusion that we can make on the evidence available to us, is pure conjecture.

It is true that Maynard Harrison does seem the likeliest candidate, but that is because we are presented with a young man of rather unpleasant character who was one of the last people to have seen Lucy Sands alive. However, there is no reason why it should not have been done by someone whose name appears in none of the accounts. Or for that matter, why not Lucy's grandmother, Sarah Stewart, whose indifference to Lucy's disappearance and lavish display of remorse and grief at news of the girl's death don't quite tally?

Perhaps it was simply too hard for the people of a small town to accept that the crime would go unsolved. Even in our fiction, we like our crimes to be cracked and feel cheated if our detective fails to find the culprit.

In an effort to winkle out the killer, Mr Liddell, the Chief Constable of Cumberland and Westmorland, passed on the following information to the men on his force:

> I am directed by the Secretary of State, with reference to your letter of the 9th ult., to inform you that in the case of the murder of Lucy SANDS, a reward of £100 will be paid by the Government to any person other than a person belonging to a police force in the United Kingdom who shall give such information and evidence as shall lead to the discovery and conviction of the murderer or murderers; and the Secretary of State will advise the grant of Her Majesty's gracious pardon to any accomplice not being the person who actually committed the murder who shall give such evidence as shall lead to a like result.

Despite a prize of the equivalent of two years' average salary, the murderer of Lucy Sands was never found. Lucy Sands' remains are somewhere in St John's churchyard in Workington, although all traces of where her grave might be have gone.

Of course her killer, whoever that was, must also now be long dead. It would be fascinating if we could discover who really was responsible.

Chapter 18

Hugh Grant, Child Killer
1882

Hugh Grant is the name of a well-known actor who has appeared in films such as *Four Weddings and a Funeral* and *About a Boy*. However, a century before the modern-day actor became famous his namesake was being tried for the murder of his own daughter.

The Hugh Grant of our story is not the movie star, whose only known crime is to have been caught *in flagrante* with a certain Divine Brown on Sunset Strip in Los Angeles – a crime deemed to be 'lewd behaviour'. Our Hugh Grant is a child-killer. A habitual drunkard, he had already treated his young wife badly and was obviously incapable of sustaining any kind of work or relationship for any period of time, although he must have had some kind of charm.

Mary McGowan had been a servant in Grant's father's house. She had already had a child by him when they married on 19 December 1881. He had already separated from her the following March, despite the fact that she had now had his second child. That same spring, he enlisted in the army, but was already back in Workington by the end of September and had lined up a job at the Derwent Works.

As with any account of an event, the witnesses gave slightly different versions of what happened at the trial; piecing together what was said, we can ascertain that within days of his return home, Grant was at loggerheads with Mary again. He had been drinking heavily, although witnesses stated he wasn't drunk, he '...had a little sup of drink about him, but not much,' according to Katie Stephenson, one of the Grant family servants. However, these were witnesses for the prosecution and they may well have thought that drunkenness might have been seen as an excuse for Grant's actions and that he might not have received the full weight of the law had they said he was drunk. Drunkenness was certainly the excuse his mother gave for his behaviour when she was cross-examined.

He was already making a commotion on Senhouse Street, singing *Home, Sweet Home* at 10.30 on the evening of 3 October 1882 when his mother sent out Katie Stephenson to get him to come home for some supper. Whilst he was sitting at the table, his mother told him that Mary, who was now living back at her parents' house, was in poor financial circumstances and feared ending up in the workhouse ('the union').

With that, Grant stormed out of his parents' house to the McGowans' house, a little two-up, two-down in Clay Flatts, where he proceeded to cause quite a fuss. In the kitchen at Clay Flatts were several members of the McGowan family. His mother-in-law, Margaret McGowan and his wife Mary were there, along with Mrs McGowan's three other children and his own two. Mary's mother told the court Grant said, 'What are you looking at, three eyes?' to which she replied, 'Let us have a cup of tea, Hugh, in peace.' And he retorted, 'You don't deserve one!'

According to reports he 'jostled the table' and seemed to be looking for some kind of altercation. When the McGowan women said that they wanted to be left in peace, the swaying Grant simply lay down by the fire and told them he was going to sleep.

It all might have ended there, but there must have been some kind of long-standing dispute between the two families. Soon after Grant had settled on the hearth to sleep off the beer, his mother arrived, accompanied by Katie Stephenson, and began swapping insults with Mary.

'May the curse of God light upon you Mary McGowan, for what you have done to my son,' Mrs Grant is reported as saying, although what the girl is supposed to have done to her son, we have no idea. The slight is probably imagined as much as real – my guess is that Grant was an indulged Mummy's Boy, who had to have his own way no matter what.

When Mary swore back at his mother, Grant jumped up again

and hit his wife, who had a child sitting on her lap at the time. According to Mrs McGowan's evidence, Grant hit his wife 'on the face with his open hand. He struck her then on the mouth, and continued to strike her five or six times about the head, face and body.' Katie Stephenson (who refers to Hugh Grant as 'Hughie' in her testimony) reports that Mary picked up a poker from the hearth to defend herself and caught Grant a glancing blow, which obviously fuelled his rage.

Mary's sister Alice whisked the child away and alerted her father, who was asleep upstairs. Then Grant lashed out at Mrs McGowan Snr, who ran out into the street to find a policeman. As his father-in-law, John McGowan, came into the kitchen, Grant punched him so hard, he fell over and then began kicking him, at which point Mary picked up a tea tin and began beating Grant over the head with it. McGowan, staggered back upstairs to get dressed, before he too went out into the cold night in search of a policeman.

The fracas had by now moved into the scullery attached to the kitchen at the back of the house, where Grant continued to harangue and abuse his wife, who was by this stage screaming. From here it spilled out into the backyard, which the McGowans shared with the neighbours, the Cassidy family. Katie Stephenson and Alice McGowan, both holding children in their arms, were already in the yard, where it all must have seemed a lot safer. But Grant barrelled through, slamming Alice's head against the brick wall as he went and nearly making her spill baby Eleanor.

It is hard to imagine that there might have been an impartial eyewitness to all this, but there was. In those days, the blast furnaces of Workington lit the night sky and the McGowans' next-door neighbour, Sarah Cassidy had been disturbed by the rumpus next door. Following the action from her own scullery window, she was able to tell the court that Grant

> ... *struck Alice McGowan, either on the side of the face or the shoulder. He then caught hold of the baby by the bottom of its dress, gave it a swing to his left shoulder, and gave it a blow on the boards three times, swinging it up and down three times. Its head struck the boards. The boards were lying by the wash house side, and were pump*

box boards. They had been lying there some time, and were about a foot high from the ground... When he struck the child against the boards he appeared to do it with great force.

Her testimony differs only slightly from that of Katie Stephenson, whose version of events has Grant swinging the child round and throwing her onto the hen-house roof. However, the surgeon involved later in examining the dead child, a Mr Ormerod from Workington, who had conducted the post-mortem examination a couple of days after the murder along with a Dr Highet, and who had been called to examine the child on the night of the killing, was of the opinion that the child's skull had been crushed.

Mr Shee's summing-up of the defence was impassioned and florid. He cast doubt on the Cassidys' story and questioned how she could see the back-yard events from the light of the furnaces. He also suggested that doctors aren't always right. His summing-up was so lengthy, that one juryman fainted during it. He also stressed that Hugh Grant's life lay in their hands and that if they made a mistake, they would be sending a man to his own death, as the *Maryport Advertiser* reported:

He pleaded before them for a fair and for a safe trial. It would be no use suggesting to them that life would be happier for this man than death. The cup of bitterness was full to overflowing, but in murder trials they must act safely. He asked them to bear in mind that no weapon was used, and that the prisoner had been peaceable and asleep, and had never raised his hand until his mother had been cursed. He urged that their verdict should be no more than manslaughter.

The jury took fifteen minutes to reach a verdict. They declared Hugh Grant to be guilty of the crime, but also asked for a recommendation of mercy. According to the *Maryport Advertiser*, the judge summed up thus:

His Lordship, assuming the black cap, said: Hugh GRANT, you have been found guilty, and most properly found guilty, by the jury, of the offence laid to your charge – the crime of wilful murder. It would have been impossible for the jury in the discharge of their duty to have found any other verdict against you. They have been good enough to add to their just verdict a recommendation for mercy. I have refrained, in mercy to you, from any inquiry into the grounds of that recommendation. That recommendation will be forwarded to the proper quarter. I earnestly urge upon you to place no reliance upon the recommendation to mercy which has been made on your behalf.

I will not say unnecessarily one word that can add to your present pain, or embitter your feelings; I will make no comment upon the crime of which you have been found guilty; I will say nothing as to the circumstances. I merely urge you, not as your judge, but as your fellow creature, to make good use of the short time remaining to you, and earnestly to prepare for the great change which is to come upon you. Seek mercy, and seek it earnestly, where alone mercy is to be found; seek it at the hands of the all merciful Redeemer.

The sentence I have to pass upon you is not my sentence; it is the sentence of the law, and a sentence which it is my duty to pass upon you; and that is, that you be taken to the place whence you came, and thence to the place of execution, and that you be there hanged by the neck until you die, and that your body be buried within the precincts of the gaol in which you have been last confined previous to your death, and may the Lord have mercy upon your soul.

The prisoner, who had been sobbing loudly for some time, was removed from the dock in a state bordering upon madness, and for some minutes after he had disappeared in charge of the gaoler his cries could be heard in the court.

So, did Grant show any remorse for what he had done? According to Katie Stephenson, 'we went away together to Grant's father's house. Shortly after we got there Hughie came in and said, "God forgive me for what I have done," and as he was lighting his pipe he said he could prepare himself for the rope in the morning. He then went out.'

Whilst there is no doubt that murdering a tiny, month-old baby was a monstrous crime, it was not premeditated. However, there were few to commiserate with Grant on the position in which he had placed himself. Besides, the judge in his summing-up to the jury before they retired to deliberate, stated clearly that, 'They must remember that wilful murder did not require any planning or scheming. Any killing in law was wilful murder.' Looking at what took place on this night, what conceivable circumstance was there which could reduce the crime from wilful murder to manslaughter?'

The *Maryport Advertiser*, making reference to the murder of Lucy Sands (see Chapter 17), certainly didn't feel that Grant had got anything other than his just desserts. The following editorial appeared in the paper on the same day as the trial report:

> *The conviction of Hugh GRANT for the wilful murder of his child at Workington was a forgone conclusion. It was impossible for the jury to return any other verdict than the one which has produced such a profound sensation in West Cumberland. No more painful task can be imposed on any person than to assist in sending a human being to the scaffold; but the men who were called upon to decide on Wednesday whether GRANT had or had not committed the most serious crime known to the law had no alternative.*
>
> *To their verdict they appended a recommendation to mercy, which will, no doubt, receive from the Home Secretary the consideration to which it is entitled. It is difficult to understand why such a recommendation should have been made. Probably it was due to the horror felt by the jurymen at dooming a fellow creature to die by the hand of the hangman. We can sympathise with this feeling, and to a certain extent, admire it, but it can only be justified on the ground we have stated.*
>
> *A fouler or more brutal crime than that of which GRANT has been convicted was never committed. There is not a shadow of an excuse for it. Mr SHEE, who defended the prisoner, struggled hard against the evidence for the prosecution, but from the first the struggle was hopeless. No eloquence, no persuasion, no pleading could disprove the damning fact that the prisoner had, without the slightest shadow of provocation, taken away the life of a helpless and unoffending infant whom it was his duty to protect, and whose very defencelessness ought to have been its best safeguard.*
>
> *The surrounding circumstances are quite insufficient to explain away the conduct of GRANT, and they do not in the slightest degree palliate his crime.*
>
> *Inflamed by passion and maddened by drink, he went down to the house of his wife's father with the deliberate intention of picking a quarrel with the inmates. He fancied himself an injured man, but for*

any injury which he had sustained he seems to have been purely responsible. His conduct when he reached the house, before he committed the terrible crime for which he has forfeited his life, was bad enough. He seems to have acted like a Malay running a-muck, and to have struck right and left at anyone near him. If, during the quarrel between them, he had killed his wife, a jury would probably have had no difficulty in reducing the crime to manslaughter. But what he did was to take his own child who had given him no cause of offence, and beat out its little life.

The Crime of GRANT has not stirred the people of this district so deeply as the murder of LUCY SANDS. The mystery in which the death of LUCY SANDS was shrouded had a great deal to do with the intense excitement which the discovery of her body created. It was both strange and frightful that a young woman should be killed and buried beneath a heap of stones not many yards from a human dwelling and near to a thickly populated town. But the murderer of LUCY SANDS was not guilty of a worse offence than that of Hugh GRANT has been convicted. And if the crime has failed to impress the public mind as deeply as the other, it is because the public has failed to grasp in its entirety the enormity of GRANT's offence.

For a strong man to attack one weaker than himself is a cowardly act, and Englishmen have always accounted it so. To assault a woman is more cowardly still. But for a father to take away the life of his own child, and stifle the feeble wail of infancy by ruffian and unprovoked violence, is a crime so appalling that no language that was ever written or spoken could depict it in its true colours.

So, you can see, there was moral rectitude aplenty, even back then. As to where the author had decided that the good people of Malaya were forever running amuck with arms flailing, one can only guess.

Grant was to get his recommendation to mercy, though, despite what the moralist of the *Maryport Advertiser* might have hoped. The *Whitehaven News* reported on 16 November 1882 under the headline 'The Workington Murder – Respite of Grant':

During the latter part of last week, a very numerously-signed petition was got up in Workington, praying for the reprieve of the convict Grant. The petition was duly forwarded to the authority, and there was a general expectation that the last dread sentence of the law could be avoided. On Tuesday morning the Carlisle newspaper gave publicity to the particulars of the date of the execution, which was fixed for Tuesday November 21st. On Monday a letter was received from Grant by his father, which showed he was penitent, though still hopeful of a reprieve. Last Tuesday morning another letter was received, this time from Mr Haverfield, the governor of Carlisle gaol, stating that he had received an intimation from the Home Office that Grant was respited during her Majesty's pleasure. The news set Grant's mother almost beside herself with joy, and his father and sister were equally gratified at the pleasing intelligence, which was soon spread throughout the town, and caused considerable satisfaction. It seems that the preliminary arrangements had been made for the execution, which was originally intended to have taken place on Monday, but Marwood having other arrangements for that day, the day following was that fixed upon for the execution. The death sentence will not be carried out. We learnt by Telegraph last night that the sentence of death has been commuted to one of penal servitude for life.

Grant could consider himself extremely lucky.

Chapter 19

The Monocled Mutineer
1920

I t was the kind of thing you might come across at Boot Hill in the Wild West, but hardly what you'd expect in a rural hamlet in Cumberland. The last thing that the worshippers at evensong expected was a shoot-out in the churchyard. But that's exactly what happened on the night of 6 June 1920.

The gunfight in the graveyard of the compact church of St John the Evangelist at Plumpton, five miles north of Penrith, left one man slumped against a gravestone. Given the dead man's eye with a gun and willingness to use it, the other four men could count themselves lucky that they were unharmed.

The dead man was Percy Topliss, although his name is sometimes spelled as Toplis. This uncertainty of spelling is somehow fitting for a man who enjoyed taking on a variety of different disguises and whose death was to leave as many questions unanswered as answered.

Plumpton church – the scene of a gun-battle in which Percy Topliss was shot.

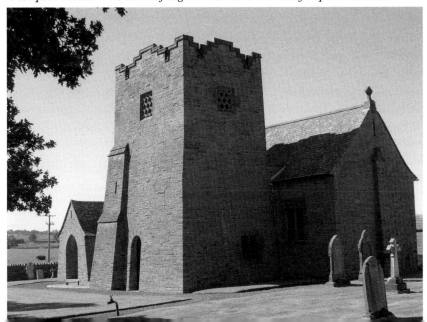

Carlisle Castle, where Percy Topliss stopped for a drink in the officers' mess, before setting out on his walk towards Penrith.

Topliss had been the subject of a nationwide manhunt that was inevitably going to result in his death; if not from a bullet, certainly at the end of a rope. His story is one of crimes escalating until murder and attempted murder were almost routine.

Topliss began his criminal life early. He was born in Chesterfield in August 1896. His parents were Herbert Topliss and the wonderfully named Rejoice Elizabeth Topliss, whose maiden name had been Webster. One can't imagine that Rejoice Elizabeth particularly rejoiced at the birth of her son, given that she was soon passing him round relatives and Francis Percy Topliss spent most of his younger days being brought up by his grandparents.

His first known brush with the law came when he obtained two suits under false pretences in Mansfield. He was given six strokes of the birch, which was obviously either no deterrent or possibly even spurred him on to further crimes. Any chance he had of holding down a job was lost when he was found drinking in a local pub instead of working the night shift in the smithy at Blackwell Colliery. By 1911, he was in trouble with the law again – this time in Scotland, where he was imprisoned for ten days for not paying a rail fare. The following year, his imprisonment was for something a little more serious – the attempted rape of a fifteen-year-old girl.

He also got a longer sentence, serving two years in gaol before enlisting in the Royal Army Medical Corps. The war years were tough for everyone, but Topliss was extremely unlucky when it came to illness, or he was particularly good at passing himself off as having the symptoms. During his tours of duty, which included Loos, Gallipoli, Bombay and Egypt, he managed to contract dysentery and malaria. By 1918, he had deserted and was then arrested and, at Nottingham Assizes, sent down for two years for fraud. During his time in the army, he also developed his ability to impersonate people from different walks of life, often passing himself off as an officer, with the aid of a gold-rimmed monocle.

On his release from prison, he was still in theory a deserter, but he somehow managed to re-enlist in the army, this time in the Royal Army Service Corps. Stationed at Bulford in Wiltshire at the Motor Transport Depot, he had plenty of access to goods that he was then able to sell illicitly, including petrol.

Some of this petrol seems to have been sold to taxi drivers around the area of Salisbury Plain. One of the local taxi drivers was Sidney George Spicer. It is likely that he knew Topliss, although there is nothing to indicate that Spicer bought illicit fuel. Spicer was found dead in Thruxton Woods near Andover on the evening on 24 April 1920 and Topliss was reported absent without leave hours later.

The authorities quickly linked the two events. Perhaps it was a deal gone wrong. Perhaps Spicer was intending to turn Topliss over to the authorities. Perhaps he was simply a witness to some other crime. It is even possible that Spicer's death was nothing to do with Topliss. However, Percy was once again in trouble and, although the authorities couldn't find him, he was tried *in absentia* and found guilty of murder.

The hunt was on to find Topliss and the *Police Gazette* of the time carried the following notice:

For murder of a taxi-cab driver - Francis Edmondson, aliases Percy Francis, Bennison, William Wilson, Jones, Topley, Taylor and Pte. Percy Francis Toplis.

Reg .No. E.M.T. 54262, M.T. R.A.S.C., Bulford Camp, C.R.O. No. S/139484, age 24 (looks older), 5ft 7in., c. fresh, h. lt. brown, slight fair ginger moustache (may now be clean shaven), e. blue, fair eyebrows, mole under chin, scar back rt. hand, believed 2 teeth missing front upper jaw, and bottom teeth false, medium build.

May be posing as an officer of the Royal Air Force, or dressed as a civilian in a smart blue serge suit.

Very plausible and bombastic. On occasions wears a gold-rimmed monocle. Believed to be in possession of a No. 6 Webley revolver.

Native of Chesterfield.

Pre. con. of fraud, larceny, and attempted rape at Mansfield, Chesterfield, Alford (Lincs) - (Percy Toplis), Annan - (Francis Edmunson), Pateley Bridge - (William Dennison), and Nottingham - (Percy Francis Toplis alias John Henry Williams).

May be found at soldiers' hostels, hotels, boarding houses, etc.

In fact, Topliss was by this time in Scotland, hiding out in the middle of wild countryside. On 1 June 1920, John Grant, a farmer working the land in a remote corner of Scotland, near Tomintoul, saw smoke coming from what he knew to be an unused bothy near a place called Well of the Lecht. He went to fetch the police, and returned later with a local constable George Greig and John Mackenzie, a gamekeeper. To begin with, Topliss tried to talk his way out of the situation, adopting an American accent and stating that he had recently been demobbed from the United States Army. Failing to convince the three men, he opened fire on all three of them, wounding Grant in the stomach and Greig in the shoulder. Then, cool as you like, whilst John Mackenzie went in search of further back-up, he collected all his personal belongings together, including his famous monocle, and hopped onto his bicycle. It is reported that as he pedalled away, he sang the famous Great War favourite *Goodbyee* over his shoulder.

On the run again, Topliss decided that Scotland was no longer

Penrith Police Station – the police party set off from here, having been issued with their revolvers.

safe for him. He abandoned his bicycle in Aberdeen and took a train to Carlisle. Once in Carlisle, he is known to have entered the castle at Carlisle, where he took tea, most probably in the officers' mess.

On 6 June 1920, Topliss left Carlisle on foot, heading for Penrith. He had almost reached Low Hesket on the A6, when he was spotted by the local constable, Alfred Fulton who noticed that he was wearing 'partial military dress'. Fulton questioned the man, but his suspicions were only mildly aroused. However, when he checked the particulars of wanted men back at the Station, he found that the man he'd seen matched Topliss's description. He set off back up the road on his bicycle to take another look. The suspicious stranger had now reached High Hesket. This time, instead of answering any of Fulton's questions, Topliss took out his Webley revolver and threatened to shoot him.

Fulton rode off quickly, exchanged his bicycle for a motorbike and sped to Penrith to the police headquarters. Here, Inspector William Ritchie and Sergeant Robert Bartram were issued with Webley revolvers. All three policemen dressed in civilian clothes and went to the *Crown Hotel,* where they borrowed a car and a driver.

Somehow or other, the Chief Constable's son, Norman de Courcy Parry, had heard about the incident and he joined the chase, riding on his motorbike. De Courcy Parry was armed with a Belgian pistol that was a 'spoil of war'. Just north of Plumpton, they spotted Topliss, overtook him to get a good look at him, then as they doubled back, Topliss ran for the cover of the gravestones in the churchyard.

It's not entirely clear what happened next. The official version has it that Topliss fired first and that the police replied with three shots, one of which hit Topliss in the chest and was to prove fatal. There's no reason to doubt this, although it is difficult to tell who actually fired the shot that killed the Monacled Mutineer.

There still remains about the incident the smell of a cover-up. This was an enormous manhunt for a minor killer and the actual murder conviction *in absentia* would nowadays be considered 'unsafe'. The behaviour of Norman de Courcy Parry seems strange. Yes, it is possible that he was simply a Hooray Henry looking for a little adventure. Indeed, it is widely believed that Norman de Courcy Parry threw his revolver into a river after the incident. One also has to ask to what extent his father, the Chief Constable of Cumberland and Westmorland Police, Charles de Courcy Parry, was aware of what had taken place.

Meanwhile, de Courcy Parry Snr and the Police Committee awarded £10 to Sergeant Bertram and Inspector Ritchie, and £15 to PC Fulton. All were awarded the King's Police Medal. Of course, de Courcy Parry Jnr couldn't be awarded anything. Was this a cover-up for his son's actions? £10 was a lot of money to a serving policeman – did it buy silence? Of course, this is only conjecture, but conjecture is the inevitable outcome when one investigates the case of Francis Percy Topliss. Given the vagueness and mystery of the entire affair and our affection for anti-heroes, it is hardly surprising, therefore, that various theories and interpretations have been thrown up surrounding the case.

Most famously, in 1986, the BBC showed a series entitled *The*

Etaples-sur-Mer – site of a famous mutiny in the First World War. Some accounts of Topliss's adventures maintain that he was heavily involved in the mutiny, but it seems it is unlikely he was even there.

Monocled Mutineer, based on a book by William Allison and John Fairley, that was to cause a furore. Written by the great Alan Bleasdale, who was also responsible for such classic television as *The Boys from the Black Stuff* and *GBH*, it depicted the adventures of Percy Topliss as essentially an anti-establishment ruffian, playing the system at its own foolish game and unwilling to join in the madness of the slaughter in Flanders. The programme was heavily criticised by Conservative right-wingers and caused ructions between the Government of the day and the BBC and so gained a much wider audience than serious dramas normally garner.

It also gave Topliss a prominent role in the mutiny at Etaples. Etaples, on the coast of Northern France, is a small fishing port, not far from the more up-market resort of Le Touquet. During the First World War, Etaples served as a base and a hospital for wounded. New recruits and men hardened from weeks on the front line were forced to drill on the sand-dunes, often regardless of their state of health. Conditions were such that some kind of flare-up

Penrith Town Hall – the inquest into Topliss's death was held here.

was inevitable. Matters came to a head in September 1917, when a soldier who had walked across the sands into the town of Etaples itself returned late, because he had miscalculated the tides and was arrested for being a deserter by over-zealous Military Police, who were probably trying to keep the lid on what was a bubbling cauldron. Although there was some shooting, it would seem that the mutiny was largely confined to demonstrations and refusals to co-operate. Persuasion to return to normality was brought about by the deployment of a machine-gun squadron. One man was executed for his part in the mutiny, a Corporal Jesse Short of the Northumberland Fusiliers. The files on the mutiny remain closed until its 100th anniversary in 2017, so we must wait for the full story to emerge, but the 'mutiny' seems to have been more of a minor uprising than a full-scale revolt.

Many historians doubt that Topliss was even involved in the mutiny, let alone in Etaples at the time. However, it is difficult to know exactly where he was at any given moment, as he was so prone to assume aliases. The likelihood is that he was simply on a troop-ship bound for India.

Whilst Bleasdale's Topliss is a figure who enables us to see much of the folly of the war, the real Percy Topliss seems a far less likeable character. He is far more villain than loveable rogue. Whilst one might argue that he was a victim of his background, he was still a rapist and murderer.

As for the famous monocle, it is now in Penrith Museum. Topliss's belongings were given to the Board of Guardians in Penrith to pay for his funeral. They handed over the monocle to the museum, where you can visit it to this day. Finding Topliss's grave is a little harder. He is buried in Penrith, in an unmarked grave in Beacon Edge Cemetery. The vicar of Christ Church insisted that Topliss be buried with full Christian dignity on the basis that he'd never been judged properly on earth, so therefore was fully entitled to such a ceremony.

On 8 June, just two days after he had been killed in the churchyard at Plumpton, the inquest was held at Penrith Town Hall. It took the jury three minutes to return a verdict that Topliss was killed justifiably.

Chapter 20

The Borrowdale Garrotting 1928

Grange-in-Borrowdale, 19 June 1928. A local farmer, Thomas Wilson, was returning home after a day's work. His route took him through Cummacatta (sometimes spelled Cumma Catta) Wood, overlooking Derwentwater, where he saw an open umbrella lying on the grass, beneath which was stretched out a finely-dressed Chinese lady.

He knew vaguely who the lady was as he had already heard on the grapevine that she was one half of a Chinese couple who had booked into the *Borrowdale Gates Hotel*. Back in the 1920s, it would have been unusual to find Chinese visitors in the area. More limited travel opportunities and a far less diverse national culture meant that any foreigners, especially those who were visibly foreign, tended to attract attention.

For many the typical, indeed stereotypical, Chinese man or woman would have been someone who worked in a sweaty laundry, such as the Mr Wu of the George Formby song *Limehouse Laundry Blues* which came out only four years after the events in this story. They certainly wouldn't have expected a near-aristocratic pair of Chinese, who were well-dressed, educated and affluent. So it was that word had spread about the novelty of a real Chinese couple spending their honeymoon in the area. The honeymooning couple was Chung Yi Miao and his bride of only a few days, Wai Sheung Sui, whose dress and manner exuded education and breeding.

Later, when Wilson got to his local, he happened to mention that he had seen the oriental lady, who was already the talk of the neighbourhood, resting in the grass. At the bar, as he told his story, was a Southport-based policeman called William Pendlebury, who

The Borrowdale Gates Hotel, *Chung Yi Mao and his bride Wai Sheung Sui stayed here whilst on their honeymoon in the Lake District. Chung Yi Mao's stay lasted just a little longer than his wife's.*

simply happened to be on holiday in the village. Unconvinced that the woman would be lying alone in the grass in weather that was chilly for the time of year, he set off with Wilson to find her, fearing she might be ill.

When Pendlebury and Wilson reached Cummacatta Wood, they found that the lady stretched out under the umbrella was more than just ill. At first sight, it looked as though she had been sexually assaulted and then garrotted with three lengths of cord. A team consisting of Inspector Harry Graham of the Keswick Police, Ralph Mayson, a photographer, and a Dr Crawford arrived soon after. They established that she had also been robbed. Marks on her ring finger hinted that rings had been taken from the body, although strangely enough, she still wore a diamond-encrusted watch.

They also thought that the fact that poor Wai Sheung Sui's dress had been lifted up beyond her breasts was deliberately meant to indicate some kind of sexual angle to the crime, although she had not actually been sexually assaulted.

They immediately suspected that it was Chung who had killed Sheung Sui. Even in those days, the police knew that a married woman was far more likely to be killed by her husband than anyone else. Nowadays, it is also well known that killers who know their victims often attempt to cover up their crime in such a way as to lead the police astray. 'Staged' murders often involve attempting to misdirect the police as to the motive of the crime. Back then, it must surely have been as much 'hunch' as deductive reasoning.

When they arrived at the hotel to tell Chung of his wife's death, they became convinced that it was him from the first few words he spoke to them. Summoned from his bed and told that his wife had been robbed and garrotted Chung is reported as saying, 'It's terrible! My wife assaulted, robbed and murdered.' No mention had been made of the apparent sexual nature of the crime, heightening suspicion. He then went on to ask the bizarre question 'Had she knickers on?'

He was taken to the police station in Keswick, whilst the bedroom that he and his bride had occupied was searched. In it, they found a jewel case containing around £3,500-worth of items, which was an absolute fortune, especially when you bear in mind that a railway clerk would have earned around £4.00 per week, and possibly even then envied by other workers. Whilst the selling of the jewels might have provided some kind of flimsy motive, it didn't amount to any kind of real evidence. However, the police did find two clues that would eventually lead to Chung's conviction. Having ransacked the bedroom, they were unable to find the rings taken from the body, but one of the policemen happened upon a couple of rolls of undeveloped film. They were passed on to the local photographer to be developed to see if there was anything on them that might be of use. When the photographer peeled away the wrapper, he found the missing rings.

Then, on top of the wardrobe was more compelling evidence. Amongst the small sheets of paper found there was one that read, in Mandarin: 'Be sure to do it on the ship. Don't do it on the ship. Again, consider on arrival in Europe.'

Chung admitted that he had written these words, but could not explain to the police what they meant. Later, in court, they were to prove to be one of the most damning pieces of evidence, interpreted as showing that he had been planning the crime for some time and that only the location was in doubt.

Meanwhile, the police set about interviewing the owner, staff and guests at the hotel in order to piece together the events of that day. The owner, Miss Crossley, proved extremely helpful and was able to be very precise about what had happened. With information gathered from different sources, the police were soon able to account for most of Chung's movements.

The previous day, the young couple took breakfast and lunch in the hotel, then went out for a walk at around 4 o'clock. June in the Lake District is not always the warmest time of year and no-one was particularly surprised that Chung should be wearing an overcoat. However, only Chung returned at around four o'clock. He explained his wife's absence by saying that she was finding the weather slightly colder than expected and had gone into Keswick to buy warmer underclothes.

In the evening, Sheung Sui had still not returned and Chung ate alone in the dining-room, saying that his wife would return later, he was sure and that he was not worried. When she still hadn't arrived by the end of dinner, Miss Crossley, knowing that the shops had been shut several hours, was extremely anxious and asked Chung if she should go out to meet the bus from Keswick. Chung insisted that it wasn't necessary and that his wife would arrive by private car. Nevertheless, Miss Crossley went out to meet the nine o'clock bus and, obviously, Sheung Sui was not on it. Chung even went to bed alone, apparently unconcerned that his wife was still not back.

From his bizarre behaviour, the evidence they collected from his room and bloodstains on the coat he had been wearing when he went out for his afternoon walk, the police felt that they could construct a strong enough case against Chung. He was sentenced for trial at Carlisle.

At his trial, Chung tried two main prongs of defence. The first was that his poor English, together with his lisp, meant that people he had spoken to had often misunderstood him. So the sentence that convinced the police that Chung was the killer wasn't 'had she her knickers on?', but 'had she her necklace on?' He also spoke about two Chinese men they had seen in Keswick the day of their arrival in the area. He tried to place the blame firmly with them and, whilst there was some evidence that a couple of Chinese visitors had been spotted in Keswick, this was thought to be entirely coincidental.

The trial was held in front of Sir Travers Humphreys, who was later to preside over the trial of John George Haigh, the notorious acid bath murderer. Interestingly, in his years as a solicitor, Humphreys had been hired by Oscar Wilde to issue the writ against the Marquis of Queensberry, the man who invented the rules of boxing, that would eventually lead to the famous trial that put Wilde behind bars for two years.

The story was global news and the *New York Times* of 25 October 1928 carried the following headline, ensuring that it got its own local angle:

CHINESE SLEW BRIDE, ENGLISH JURY FINDS; Ex-Columbia Student Must Die for Strangling Wife on Honeymoon in June. CHUNG ASSERTS INNOCENCE Valuable Jewels of Wealthy Oriental Merchant's Daughter Were Missing From Body.

The evidence against Chung had built up slowly and, whilst none of it individually was enough to convict him, cumulatively it pointed inexorably to his guilt. When the jury brought in a guilty verdict, after deliberating for just an hour, Chung screamed at Sir Travers Humphreys and the jury that he had been dealt with most unfairly.

Something in Chung's pride had obviously been pricked. He even took it upon himself to conduct his own defence at the appeal hearing, held a few weeks later, where the story even made the pages of *Time Magazine* for Monday 3 December, where they reported:

> *The Lord Chief Justice of England, Baron Hewart, heard last week in London the appeal of one Chung Yi-miao, a Chinese law student whom a lower English court had sentenced to hang for murdering his Chinese wife, also a young student.*
>
> *Murderer Chung pleaded his own appeal before the Lord Chief Justice. When judgment was about to be pronounced, Chung Yi-miao leaned forward and cupped his hand behind his ear, in order not to miss a word.*
>
> *Imposing in great wig and majestic robes, Baron Hewart said: 'It is impossible to say that there is not ample evidence to find that this appellant committed this crime. Miao is guilty of a diabolical, calculated crime. This appeal is dismissed.'*

Chung was hanged at Strangeways Prison in Manchester on 6 December 1928. His wife of a few weeks, Wai Sheung Sui, was buried in the churchyard at St Kentigern's church. Her body didn't rest here very long, however. About a year after her interment, relatives arranged to have her body exhumed and repatriated to Macao. As it was, she briefly shared a resting place with a former Poet Laureate, Robert Southey, whose greatest gift to literature was the story of the *Three Bears* (no Goldilocks then, just a wicked old woman nicking porridge) and Sir Edmund Henderson, who founded Scotland Yard's CID.

But who were the two Chinese visitors who had arrived from America on an elongated honeymoon that would end in tragedy? Chung and Wai Sheung Sui had met the previous October in New York. Wai's father, a wealthy merchant from Macao, had died a few years before and Wai was in the United States to sell off some of his

St Kentigern's Church, Crosthwaite, Keswick – the body of Wai Sheung Sui was buried here, but exhumed for repatriation by her family a year or so later.

estate, in particular jade pieces that her father had collected. She was now a young lady of some fortune, who had also been educated at university – at a time when university education for women, although no longer uncommon, was certainly not the usual path for a young lady who could simply have lived the life of a lotus-eater on the family's money.

She was obviously infatuated with the apparent worldliness and sophistication of Chung Yi Miao. He claimed that his father was a lawyer and that he was in America, finishing his studies at Columbia University in order to have a well-rounded education and to qualify as an international lawyer himself. He alleged that he was a Mandarin Chinese – in other words that he came from a privileged background himself, although this was probably pure invention.

This wealthy couple (or at least one of them was wealthy) wanted a honeymoon to match their status. They embarked on a slow journey around parts of the United States, including Niagara Falls and Florida, before crossing the Atlantic to spend time in Scotland and England. They also planned to go on to mainland Europe to see Paris.

However, the trip was cut short in Grange-in-Borrowdale by a murder whose motive still seems unclear to this day. At the time, much was made of the gynaecological operation that Wai had undergone before the marriage. Had it made her unable to have children? In which case, not wanting to appear incapable of producing children (and thus not man enough) to friends and family, did he kill her to save face?

There is also another story, which may explain the coincidental presence of the two Chinese men in Keswick that day. There is a story that Chung was already married in China and that the men were detectives hired by Chung's original in-laws to track him down and confront him with his bigamy. It is feasible that this was the case, but it is unlikely that they killed poor Sheung Sui as, whilst they were seen in Keswick, there are no reports of their having been in Grange-in-Borrowdale, some five miles away, where Chinese visitors, as we have already seen, had a certain curiosity value.

It is possible that Chung killed for reasons of machismo, but I suspect that the motive was just plain old greed. Certain of Chung's actions during his brief engagement and even briefer marriage indicate that he had financial problems. On the honeymoon, he failed to report to the police or the issuing bank travellers' cheques that had gone missing or had been stolen. He relied heavily on his wife's money, as she drew it from her own bank accounts. He also stole the rings. Rings are small, easily concealed and easily sold, whereas the watch would have been larger to hide and more easily traceable.

The most likely explanation is that Chung had come to Britain in order to kill his wife on some point of the journey. He then stood to inherit a fortune. That an intelligent woman of obvious discernment should have been duped by him is hardly surprising. Con men are remarkably persuasive, as we have seen in other episodes in this book. If we could easily rumble them, then they simply wouldn't be con men.

However, even the trial judge, Sir Travers Humphreys was not entirely sure of Chung's motives. Mistakenly calling him 'Miao' in the belief that this was his surname, Humphreys writes in his account of the trial:

> ... the account which I read of his conduct on the appeal confirmed me in the view which I had formed during the trial on the subject of 'motive' - as did the information that he had from the beginning been the source of a great deal of trouble to his advisers. He had twice changed his solicitors and, as already stated, had at the end of his trial, in effect, charged his counsel, one of the ablest defenders on the Northern Circuit, with failing to present his case to the jury in what he regarded as the most convincing manner.
>
> The fact is, as I believe, that the legal view, which is often said to be that everyone is either sane or insane, but which is more accurately stated as assuming everyone to be responsible in law for his actions unless and until the contrary is shown, fails to take into account the large, and perhaps increasing, number of persons who, though they know what they are doing, and that they are doing wrong, are so muddle-headed, so conceited and arrogant (Miao was intensely vain of his legal accomplishments) that they lose the power of controlling their thoughts and actions. They are frequently what the world calls religious. One of the statements made by Miao to the appeal Court was that he was in the habit of asking God which of the two or more courses he should take, when he would put the alternatives on separate pieces of paper, would then pray for guidance and decide by drawing a lot.
>
> Does not that statement indicate a confusion of mind sufficient to account for almost any action? I am satisfied that Miao murdered his wife and was rightly hanged, but I was and still am quite unable to answer to my own satisfaction the question, 'Why did he do it?'

We shall never know.

Bibliography

A Book of Trials – Personal Recollections of an Eminent Judge of the High Court,
   Sir Travers Humphreys

A Census of Whitehaven, 1762

Anon *The Life of Mary Robinson, the Celebrated Beauty of Buttermere; Containing an*
   Account of the Frauds and Impositions Practised by John Hatfield, Commonly Called
   The Keswick Imposter also the Proceedings of His Trial, And an Account of His Execution

Anon *The Trial of Thomas Wallis, Ann Heslop, Thomas Leeke Wilson, John Boustead and*
   John Wilson for a Conspiracy &c. against one Jonathan Sewell

Ashbridge, Ian *Murder in Cumbria*

Bott, George *Keswick: The Story of a Lake District Town*

Eddlestone, John *The Encyclopaedia of Executions*

Gawalt, Gerard (translator & editor) *John Paul Jones' Memoir of the American*
   Revolution

Hay, Daniel *Whitehaven – An Illustrated History*

Klontz, Catherine *The Embleton Murder*

Koven, Mrs Reginald de *The Life and Letters of John Paul Jones*

Lee, Sarah *Classic Murders of the North West*

MacLeod, Innes *Sailing on Horseback – William Daniell and Richard Ayton in*
   Cumbria and Dumfries and Galloway

Officer, Lawrence H *Purchasing Power of British Pounds from 1264 to 2006,*
   Measuring Worth.com

Scott-Hindson, Brian *Whitehaven Harbour*

Stainton J M *The Reverend John Stainton, 1785-1848, clerk, incumbent curate of*
   Rampside

The Newgate Calendar

Newspapers and magazines
Lloyd's Evening Post
New York Times
The Carlisle Journal
The Carlisle Patriot
The Cumberland Magazine
The Cumberland Pacquet
The Lancaster Gazette
The Police Gazette
The Times
The Whitehaven News
Time Magazine

Index